BURIED SECRETS

BURIED SECRETS

Remembrance of Things Past – Learning to
Live with Those Unwelcome Feelings

Savi McKenzie-Smith

Matador
9 Priory Business Park,
Wistow Road, Kibworth Beauchamp,
Leicestershire. LE8 0RX
Tel: 0116 279 2299
Email: books@troubador.co.uk
Web: www.troubador.co.uk/matador
Twitter: @matadorbooks

ISBN 978 1789013 405

British Library Cataloguing in Publication Data.
A catalogue record for this book is available from the British Library.

Printed and bound in Great Britain by 4edge Limited
Typeset in 11pt Minion Pro by Troubador Publishing Ltd, Leicester, UK

Matador is an imprint of Troubador Publishing Ltd

For
Julian, Catherine
Alex, Joseph, Emma and Saish

CONTENTS

PREFACE

**What happens to our past experiences
as we approach the end of our lives?**

Well-intentioned secrets followed by lies to protect loved ones are common. Sooner or later, the collective lies disturb the emotional equilibrium. Stories of buried secrets, long forgotten, return as irrepressible feelings to haunt people's daily lives. The slate cannot be wiped clean. Our past is also our present and our future. *Buried Secrets: Remembrance of Things Past* gives a range of stories from life experiences of several older adults with long-kept secrets that disrupted their later lives. Growing old is often a time for reconciliation. This book indicates how connected feelings of guilt and grieving, and both physical and emotional losses, can be experienced at this stage of life.

Every old person was once a child, moving into adolescence before reaching adulthood. Wordsworth succinctly stated that 'The child is the father to the man', suggesting that both positive and negative aspects of the adult personality are identifiable from childhood days. Anxiety, stress, depressive states, self-harm, emotional and physical abuse may be daily experiences for many during childhood. The second part of this book attempts to explain how those undesirable experiences from formative, earlier days are woven into our personality. They often impact at some stage or may intensify as one nears the end of life.

Feelings of love, hate, anger and sadness from early years, without intention, remain in the memory, either accurately or warped by time. Often without any warning, they may be recalled and significantly disrupt our daily lives. Insightfulness, tolerance, forgiveness, remorse and integration are necessary to adapt and reconstruct a new state of mind to move forward. In this section, the excerpts taken from various stages of the lifespan show the pain, guilt and sadness that follow. However, they also indicate how one can come to terms with one's experiences and enhance the remainder of one's lifetime.

INTRODUCTION

Depression, anxiety and emotional stress are far more prevalent today than generally acknowledged. Older adults are no exception. Their numbers are rapidly expanding and are predicted to continue to do so. There has been a general reluctance for psychotherapists to work with elderly people for many reasons. Why waste time on people who are not going to live for much longer? There may be fear around thinking about one's own ageing and death. Many old people now live well into their nineties and lead productive lifestyles. Constructive provision for mental well-being, if necessary, can enhance the remainder of lifetimes as described here in the reconstituted, fictionalised stories, taken from true-life experiences. Feelings are a central part of our lives and old people are not devoid of them.

As a professional psychotherapist, my work extended to seeing depressed older adults at the Tavistock Centre, as well as within my private practice. My interest in working with older adults originated from a previous experiential study of observing old people suffering from dementia. I applied a psychoanalytic method of closely observing such people to understand their emotional needs. Dementia, which is still very much beyond medical control, stems from organic, degenerative, physical processes. Although this may also be true of severe depression, much of the milder states of emotional dysfunction stem from irrepressible, disturbing feelings that are recalled from memory. Intolerable experiences may have been suppressed or repressed and denied at the time, but never got rid of. 'Shelved' in their original form, the experiences remain in the mind. Remembrance of past events may frequently or infrequently be recalled. What the mind does with them depends on the individual's capacity to process them.

This book aims to create some awareness for the lay reader of any age that support for emotional disturbances in later life is available and does help. The first part of the book reviews the impact of some very disturbing feelings in older adults and how psychotherapy helped them. The second part of the book aims at creating an awareness for those who wish to learn more of our inner life, professionally referred to as the 'psyche' or the unconscious, or in the terminology of Sigmund Freud (1), the pioneer of psychoanalysis, as 'unconscious processes'. Vignettes and excerpts from other age groups, adopting a similar style, are given to clarify the various states of mind. Depression can be controlled by antidepressants, which alleviate the condition but do not get to the root of the problem. They have side effects, but this does not mean that psychotherapy does not have any other impact. During the process, the patient/client may 'act out' his feelings outside the consulting room, if not held by the psychotherapist, as explained in Section Two.

It is now generally accepted that as one grows older, one recalls and remembers some of those early experiences. Past, good experiences are once more enjoyed. However, negative, disturbing or hostile experiences, as well as secrets and lies, perhaps long forgotten, also reoccur from memory and disturb one's equilibrium. Bearing in mind that all remembrances of the past may not be accurate or the reality, an attempt is made to describe some of the disturbing feelings experienced, particularly by older adults. Growing old and nearing the end of their existence instigated the urge to reconsider these feelings, some of which were displayed in unexpected ways.

Emotional difficulties are not restricted to older people. Therapy with other age ranges are discussed in the second part of the book, so as to clarify the earlier thinking of Freud's contributions and the ever-growing thoughts on the subject. Living in a competitive, materialistic world can be stressful and challenging for the young as well as the old. Perhaps these pages will help the many people suffering in silence to seek support. Treatment for emotional problems is more available and although much of the stigma attached has been eradicated, difficulties still prevail in seeking help. Words with the prefix 'psycho' – psychology, psychotherapy, psychoanalysis, psychiatry – create confusion as to the direction one should seek for help. This book attempts to clarify some of this and explain how psychotherapy offers to alleviate depression and distressing feelings. The truth, however negative or painful, cannot be eradicated. Acceptance and integration rather than denial can be achieved, giving one a feeling of wellbeing and helping to enhance one's lifestyle.

But it is also a myth to presume we are in total control, as Shakespeare – a voracious authority on emotion – succinctly reminds us in *Hamlet*:

'There is a divinity that shapes our end,
Rough hue it as you may.'

Our *destiny* is often beyond our control. Perseverance is required to move forward. Disturbing thoughts that we wish to bury forever are routinely experienced. But instead of denying them, we can think about those feelings and adjust accordingly for the better, bearing in mind that there may be pitfalls to negotiate.

A further purpose of these pages is to draw attention to the fact that, as individuals, we are like coins with two faces – the physical 'outer life' and the emotional 'inner life' – that are interdependent and coexistent. One without the other makes us become partly or wholly dysfunctional. The psychotherapist does not teach or advise, but listens, observes and creates a space as a catalyst to help the patient/client think differently. Encouragement to reassess and learn from one's experiences is the keystone of the process. This is the 'talking' cure. Universal experiences are part of human existence and play a significant role in everyone's daily life. They may create imbalance and emotional disturbances. More often, they are given less attention than physical discomfort. The general tendency is to keep one's innermost feelings and thoughts private. Within these pages, an attempt is being made to give simplified explanations of some very complicated and complex mechanisms of how we function from within.

Some people may feel they need emotional support but feel terrified or tentative about seeking support. What happens in the consulting room? Many are unable to understand how it works from an intellectual perspective because it is considered as an experiential activity. But the practitioner of psychotherapy requires an intellectual understanding of some very complicated mechanisms of the human mind. Psychotherapy training involves the capacity for learning psychoanalytical theory and using the knowledge to identify and interpret experiential activities in a more simplified form. Psychotherapists undergo years of analysis with an experienced analyst. The psychotherapist initially assesses the problems presented by the patient/client. This may present an enigma to the therapist as well as the client. Each person needs to be treated differently as they come with varying problems. The learned theories are the major tools of the psychotherapist and these are adjusted and explained to suit each patient/client's need without moving away from the reality. The psychotherapist does not instigate change but helps the patient/client to consider what changes he/she could make to better his/her lifestyle.

Encouraging the patient to observe and think about his feelings and actions is a relevant part of the process. With many, this encourages a self-awareness that creates a way of life that continues for long after the therapy ends. Exposure of one's innermost feelings may feel terrifying or even abhorrent. This attempt is not to make the profession of psychotherapy a 'peep show', but to create awareness of how it works and how one may benefit from undergoing the process. Looking inwardly at the true self is broadly getting to know and acknowledging the personality. Some people have psychotherapy to learn to cope with the pressures at home and work.

The cornerstone of this book is about the inadmissible secrets and lies of several older adults, which had been hidden throughout most of their lives. As they grew older, they felt an urge to divulge and confess their negative actions to someone who would understand them. Some felt suddenly inundated and haunted by their past activities and became depressed or had minor breakdowns. Circumstances may have necessitated such negative actions for self-preservation. However, it is also relevant to bear in mind that what has been done cannot be undone. This book is not only for those who wish to have a healthy mental lifestyle in old age, but for anyone of any age hoping to improve their emotional relationships. Stressful states of mind, which are a common feature of today, can be alleviated to a wide extent. The assumption that there is no respite for past demeanours or atrocities are not altogether true. Reassessment and adjustment are possible through the acceptance or acknowledgement of one's responsibility, and through sincerely feeling remorse to allow integration.

The stories told below were originally inspired by my work with older adults. It felt appropriate to include a chapter on how ageing and growing old impacts on the personality of many old people, especially as they become aware of the short time they have left in this world. Awareness of feelings connected with the present are more often and openly expressed. Many feel the need to make appropriate readjustments before it is too late. During therapy sessions, 'I feel sad', 'I feel so guilty', 'I wish I had not done or said…' are common statements. Being listened to in the accepting atmosphere of the consulting room encourages them to trust that they will be listened to without prejudice or criticism. Some emotional and stressful memories may initially be somatised and experienced as physical pain. Words like 'guilt', 'gratitude', 'grieving', 'remorse', 'melancholia' and 'mourning' become more common in therapy. These are very important themes, connected with everyone's lives to varying degrees, but often ignored by the young. I discovered that these concepts become more significant as one grows old. Ageing seems to be a period when recalling and remembering earlier experiences intensify and intrude upon daily life. Obviously, some of these recollections may be confused, blurred or imagined. In my work, these feelings disrupted peace of mind and therapeutic intervention supported such individuals to come to terms with the negative aspects of their selves. It helped them to regain some peace of mind.

The aim or purpose of this book is to familiarise anyone interested with how we function from a deeper level or our 'inner self'. It is an attempt to present some of the intricate theories confined to psychoanalytic literature in as simplified a form as possible. Confidentiality has been preserved and all concerned have given written consent to be in this book. I would also like to add that the old people who inspired the fruition of these pages sadly departed from this world some time ago. After many years of deliberation, I hope that by disclosing their secrets and lies many a person in a similar situation will be encouraged to seek help and learn to integrate unwanted and undesirable feelings.

The book is divided into two sections:

In Section One, the main theme is about the reconstituted, fictionalised stories of the negative activities of old people. They reflect the impact of recalling and remembering some of their early irrepressible memories. Pleasant recollections from the past can be relived and enjoyed to the fullest, but unpleasant ones can stir up emotional distress, causing anxieties that may be ignored or cause mental imbalance, leading to varying states of depression. Not everyone seeks psychotherapeutic intervention. However, for the many who do seek support, therapy plays a significant role in alleviating some of their anxieties. Some of the people with whom I worked felt overwhelmed by the unexpected intrusion into their past. Peace of mind could only be achieved when those images were made tolerable by emotionally accepting and integrating any uncomfortable feelings, regardless of whether they were the truth, confusion or reality. What mattered was that they had previously caused an immense amount of distress and mental pain. Working alongside a trained psychotherapist helped.

Creating a space where one is listened to and feels free to say whatever is going on in the mind without being made to feel ridiculous helps the recipient to make emotional and mental adjustments. Much of the distress and anxiety those individuals had been feeling were alleviated. It needs to be stressed that positive changes can only be done by the individual. The therapist acts as a catalyst, providing a space where this can be achieved. Being in therapy does not automatically mean that one can simply be rid of the past. It is a means of making the negative aspects of the personality psychically tolerable through integration. In simple terms, this means accepting one's negative aspects rather than negating them.

The older people with whom I worked felt overwhelmed by some of their secrets, which had been previously well-hidden, and how they suddenly impacted their lives at this later stage. Past behaviour that they had almost forgotten returned to torment them. Their experiences indicated the impossibility of ridding oneself of the events of one's earlier days. Guilt is a very strong factor that has to be worked through and genuine remorse felt before previous irresponsible acts can be tolerated and made emotionally bearable. The anxiety surrounding past negative activities suddenly disrupted their daily lives at this late stage. Peace of mind could only be redeemed through clinical support. This enabled the understanding of their troublesome feelings from a different perspective. Gradually, they learnt to be honest with their true self by confronting, acknowledging and integrating their wrongdoing before they acquired some emotional stability.

Section One concludes with a chapter on growing old and how early feelings may come to the fore at this late stage of a lifespan. What do I mean by 'early feelings'? As mentioned in the preface, we not only grow physically from childhood to adulthood, but we also develop emotionally. What we experience during those early years is not only our past, but our present.

Section Two explains the development of our inner or psychic life, acknowledged as the personality, in more detail. Words like 'feelings', 'memory' and 'personality' are widely used without much thought given to their true meaning. In this section, an attempt is made to explain their in-depth meaning as understood from psychoanalytic theory in as simplified a form as possible.

Included in the conclusion is a poem written by the grandson of the late Dr Hyatt Williams, at the time an adolescent. Dr Williams encouraged me to learn from my experience during my training and supervision sessions with him. He believed that if one learnt from one's own mistakes and accepted them as such, one would be able to help others understand the negative aspects of themselves.

I repeat that confidentiality and trust in the psychotherapist are essential in the profession. All examples are therefore introduced as reconstructed, reconstituted, fictional versions of older adults and others suffering from mild depression. The therapy supported them to alleviate some recalled, stressful feelings and thereby enhanced their lifetime. In Section Two, the vignettes are also reconstituted. Examples are necessary to clarify some relevant points being made to indicate how we develop our personalities from childhood and the consequences this has on our adult lives.

Desiderata – Words for Life

Go placidly amid the noise and haste,
and remember what peace there may be in silence.

As far as possible, without surrender
be on good terms with all persons.
Speak your truth quietly and clearly;
and listen to others,
even the dull and the ignorant;
they too have their story.

Avoid loud and aggressive persons, they are vexations to the spirit.
If you compare yourself with others,
you may become vain and bitter;
for always there will be greater and lesser persons than yourself.
Enjoy your achievements as well as your plans.

Keep interested in your own career, however humble;
it is a real possession in the changing fortunes of time.
Exercise caution in your business affairs;
for the world is full of trickery.
But let this not blind you to what virtue there is;
many persons strive for high ideals;
and everywhere life is full of heroism.

Be yourself.
Especially, do not feign affection.
Neither be cynical about love;
for in the face of all aridity and disenchantment
it is as perennial as the grass.

Take kindly the counsel of the years,
gracefully surrendering the things of youth.
Nurture strength of spirit to shield you in sudden misfortune.
But do not distress yourself with dark imaginings.
Many fears are born of fatigue and loneliness.
Beyond a wholesome discipline,
be gentle with yourself.

You are a child of the universe,
no less than the trees and the stars;
you have a right to be here.
And whether or not it is clear to you,
no doubt the universe is unfolding as it should.

Therefore be at peace with God,
whatever you conceive Him to be,
and whatever your labors and aspirations,
in the noisy confusion of life keep peace with your soul.

With all its sham, drudgery and broken dreams,
it is still a beautiful world.
Be cheerful.
Strive to be happy.

Attributed to Max Ehrmann, 1927

SECTION ONE

1

SECRETS AND LIES
AND MORE LIES

Many of us are afraid to indulge, let alone think about, who we are and our past to ascertain whether we behaved appropriately or not, for fear of remembering something that may be toxic. Unfortunately, as much as one tries to be rid of or to deny past unsavoury experiences, they are remembered when least expected. Recalling and remembering are normal, everyday activities for all of us and are, in general, an unavoidable experience. From my clinical experience with people of all ages and especially my work with older adults, I realised that attempting to avoid past negative memories only resulted in more mental strain. Consequently, unhappiness, anxiety, stress-related physical conditions and depression resulted. Mild depression is not obvious in many instances because it can easily be disguised by presenting a 'false front'. Feelings play a significant role and there is no escape from them, though we often do not acknowledge this fact or give it much attention.

Some depressed people busy themselves in different ways to avoid thinking about how they really feel. Many, who are unable to take the mental strain, become bodily ill. Depression is often under-diagnosed and ignored as treatment swivels around the physical conditions. Somatic associations are often overlooked, ignored or not taken into consideration. Preference for antidepressants seem to be the option to alleviate stressful conditions or mild depression. No doubt they are useful to relieve the condition but only temporarily. Avoidance of confronting the real problem can last a whole lifetime, through denying innermost feelings. However, with many, sooner or later, the *Truth* has to be acknowledged and dealt with.

At many social gatherings of older people, the conversation inevitably involves health problems. There is no reluctance to go into gory details with any form of severe physical illness. However, if keenly observed, it is usually confined to this and there is a general avoidance of discussing personal mental or emotional states. Although someone might be feeling all kinds of lurking anxieties, these are hardly ever openly discussed. Under the veneer, many may feel silently anxious, perturbed or mildly depressed but feel too ashamed or reluctant to share these feelings in public. Any form of mental affliction that affects one's emotional well-being may be regarded as weakness in not being able to cope mentally. Some older people may even have secrets that disturb them emotionally, but keep their feelings well wrapped-up until the internal pressure cannot be avoided any longer.

However, dementia – now a common ailment – is currently talked about and acknowledged as an unfortunate state of being. The obvious outer impairment cannot be avoided or hidden and sympathy towards the sufferer is generally shown. Their deteriorating cognitive skills are unquestionably accepted. But often, very little attention is given to the emotional state of the afflicted person because most people only pay attention to the external requirements and behaviour. Many onlookers do not fathom that people diagnosed with dementia may still have personal feelings or be internally mourning the loss of past activities.

A lack of awareness as to why or how the remembrance of negative experiences from our past can continually haunt us is common.

At any age, one may feel anxious, distressed or depressed for no outward or obvious reason, but fail to understand what is causing them to experience these feelings. Past unacceptable experiences or behaviour, long forgotten or perhaps thought of as well hidden, may be believed to be buried forever. When some associated event or activity suddenly triggers them off, they are recalled without any warning, causing emotional turbulence. Many people inevitably lead dual lives, an outer public self and an inner, more private, personal self – the latter of which is often kept well hidden from scrutiny by other people. These pages are therefore also intended to assure those with hidden secrets and lies that all is not futile and that they can be helped. Professional expertise within a private setting can help them to feel remorse and to integrate their unsavoury past. This often leads to enhancing the remaining lifespan. The overall intention, as explained in the introduction, is to create awareness to those who are ignorant of how psychotherapy works and the fact that it may help. I say 'may' because personal involvement in the process is vital. During therapy, the therapist acts as a catalyst to encourage positive changes, without being assertive, enabling the patient to discover the negative aspects of the self.

My enthusiasm in writing this book stems from the fact that I helped and supported many people in finding their true selves. All they needed to do was to look with 'new eyes' as suggested by Marcel Proust, to view themselves from a different perspective. Perhaps everyone should aim to understand why we behave as we do as he also suggested (explained in more detail in Section Two) that we should 'learn to dream more, to dream all the time until we get nearer the truth', instead of ignoring or trying to be rid of unwanted, disturbing visions from the past. To gain access to and understand why one reacts or behaves the way one does in the 'outer world', it is necessary to inwardly trace back to the source of the behaviour – that is, the 'inner world' or the world from where our feelings originate.

Inevitably, the lifespan has increased and many live for much longer. It is therefore time to think about understanding the stressful emotional states and the well-being of older adults. Provision for external need is more often readily available, but a lack of insight to cater for the internal state persists. Their feelings are often ignored, overlooked or misunderstood. As mentioned earlier, as one grows older, memories from earlier, past experiences, long forgotten, are revived. Many older adults become emotionally needy and even mildly depressed. Some of their unresolved past once more feels like the present, as they recall and remember bygone days. The focus of the following chapters is about the lies and secrets of older adults who began to recall and remember some of their unsavoury past. I discovered from my work with them that they felt as though they needed to talk to someone. They were reluctant to share their past with family or friends. Talking to a psychotherapist who is non-judgemental; who listens without criticism but with empathy helped them to express some of their painful and hidden feelings. This led them to appreciate the changes in themselves that led to the enhancement of the rest of their lifetimes.

Our outward behavioural patterns and the responses from intrinsically rooted sensitivity may vastly differ from the 'reality' or 'truth' because it is in juxtaposition with our cognitive processes. Spontaneous reactions and denial of the truth make us believe we are in control. This is only a myth because the reality of the experience remains with us for the rest of our lifetime. It is a falsity to believe that we are in command of our feelings. Unfortunately, there are some people who live a lifetime believing they are in control when they are really in denial of the truth. To further understand their behaviour and to give meaning to their stories, a simplified version of the functioning of the mind or our 'inner life activities' is given in some detail, in a simplified form, in Section Two.

The following two stories concern women with similar tales. Both stories are connected with lies concerning their daughters – but that is where the comparison ends. The circumstances of the first case were very different in that the couple were persuaded that what happened was the best thing for the future welfare of the child. With hindsight, this was a quick and painless solution, which the child most probably benefitted from. But the actions then taken by the adults and kept as a secret became emotionally unbearable in later life.

In the second story, the issue of morality is involved. Perhaps extramarital relationships have always been a feature among both sexes from time immemorial. Perhaps the belief that men are usually the unfaithful sex is a myth. The notion of an unfaithful woman may not seem as outrageous as when Anna was a young woman. Societal values are perhaps more relaxed and promiscuous relationships are, in some circles, more openly accepted. Nevertheless, there is some concealment from the partner, engendering negative aspects in the inner state. Consequently, inevitable lies follow to keep the truth a secret, perhaps not only from the partner but from others as well.

Some discussion and thoughts about the emotional functioning of those involved is given at the end of the stories. It is not beyond the capacity of anyone who wishes to understand to see why they behaved thus and how their inner world functioned, though presented differently in the outer world. Not many stop to think about who they are or what their purpose of being really is. Generally, life progresses either successfully, as a failure or in some acceptable manner. Most people continue to do what they do until the past feels like the present and disrupts their equilibrium.

Before repeating some of the secrets and lies disclosed by older people within the clinical setting, it is necessary to understand that all 'unconscious processes' experienced from childhood determinedly remain with the individual (see Section Two). One may disbelieve this, but, if considered carefully, why does some of our past existence – that one may wish to ignore – come back from memory? Until our last breath, our past is part of our personality or psyche, however confused, warped or outwardly negated.

During clinical work with many older people, I discovered that it takes patience and trust before hidden secrets and lies are divulged. At times when they spoke about their past activities, their behaviour did not seem as preposterous as they envisaged. Perhaps not altogether conducive, some of their behaviour had practical solutions at the time. Spontaneous and immediate reactions to painful and disruptive emotional states are more often to regain and preserve one's immediate mental state. However, when considered later, feelings occur, oscillating between the desire to be honest or to keep the activity a secret. The latter often triggers off a series of lies. During this late stage of life, unethical behaviour can lead to persecutory states of mind and instigate overwhelming feelings of guilt, anxiety and despair. Some felt haunted by their past and it disrupted the harmony of their daily lives. Their preoccupation and stressed mental states led to feelings of torment and depression.

Some of the people discussed below became mildly depressed or had emotional breakdowns. Others acted out their inner states of mind in unexpected and uncharacteristic ways. Each person had his or her story to tell, which were sometimes not as devastating or unforgivable as they thought they were. Circumstances, environment, fear, survival and other factors played a significant role that resulted in inappropriate behaviour. Nevertheless, the secrets were distressing and disrupted their lives. Often, stories involved loved ones and the feelings of guilt provoked much anxiety and distress. The thought of the nearness of death undoubtedly instigated their need to confess. They strongly indicated the necessity to come to terms with unresolved and untold experiences from the past that haunted them. They felt a desperate need to unburden themselves of troublesome memories.

The following stories relate experiences of human behaviour under unexpected circumstances. We can all be fallacious or unknowingly selfish under difficult circumstances. At some stage, the past may catch up with us. Some resilient people continue to ignore, others reassess and others disintegrate mentally and need support to achieve emotional well-being. I repeat that the nearness of approaching death plays a significant role in stirring up long-forgotten, distressing experiences. The desire to confront the *truth* and to reveal their secrets and lies becomes urgent.

The stories are presented in a fictional form to preserve

confidentiality. Furthermore, although psychoanalytic jargon is kept to a minimum, the stories below are viewed from a psychoanalytic perspective.

The Warm Cheek

Norma looked at the wedding invitation with mixed feelings. Ella was a dear friend, but she hated weddings. At thirty-five, it was no fun going to a wedding on your own, surrounded by happy couples of all ages, blissfully together. Perhaps in reality, it was very different. The wine and champagne inevitably had something to do with it. Norma sat down, gave a big sigh, filled in the acceptance card and left it by her bag to post the next day.

She and Ella studied at the same music college. These days, they met intermittently for lunch. Ella liked talking endlessly about James, her fiancé. They had met nearly two years ago at a party, which Ella had been reluctant to go to. Now, they were going to be married. Norma sighed when she thought about the dreams she and Ella had once had about becoming great concert pianists. They used to joke about being in competition with each other.

Norma sighed, tumbled into bed and switched off the bedside lamp. Dreamily, she touched her right cheek, gave a little smile and drifted into sleep. She never understood why she did this every night and sometimes thought *Silly habit*, but it always felt comforting.

After much deliberation, Norma wore a turquoise suit with matching navy-blue accessories. She looked at herself in the mirror. The reflection showed a slim woman with large, beautiful eyes. If one looked closely, however, those eyes expressed sadness. The previous brightness in them had somewhat dulled. She regretted that her parents would not be there as they were abroad.

The wedding was grand with a large gathering, as the parents on both sides were well-off business people. Ella looked radiant and Norma wondered how much the wedding gown had cost. She chatted to a few friends and acquaintances on the terrace during the champagne and canapés reception. When everyone walked into the magnificently decorated dining room, she found her table and, as usual, was seated next to a bore. After briefly acknowledging her greeting, he hardly made conversation. Instead, he passionately concentrated on his food and ate with relish. Norma smiled to herself and thought, *He is guzzling as if he's been starved for days*. Little beads of perspiration were appearing on his bald head. Smiling to herself, Norma turned to converse with the older couple on her other side. They were old friends of Ella's parents.

The food was delicious and in abundance. She looked at some of the other tables within her view. Most of the people she knew seemed engrossed in conversation, laughing and shouting over each other. She wished she was seated with some of them. She dreaded the inevitable dance when the couples would sway around, looking as if they were intoxicated with each other, which was probably more to do with the champagne and wine than love. She quickly reminded herself not to be nasty or envious. Giving a little sigh, she tried to concentrate and respond to the older woman's comments. Preoccupied thus, she almost jumped out of her chair as an arm unexpectedly rested on her shoulder. She swung around to see a tall, slim and handsome face. She squinted for a moment and then jumped up with joy and amazement. Overwhelmed by this man's presence, she exclaimed:

"Pierre, how good to see you again! I can't believe it! How did I miss seeing you? Where were you sitting?"

Pierre gave Norma a big hug and held her closely for a minute, then gently kissed her on the right cheek and led her away. This simple act opened a floodgate of memories and feelings. She felt the warmth of that kiss taking her back to when she was eight years old. Most summers, her family travelled to France to spend a few weeks with Pierre's family. They had moved there with their three young children. Their youngest daughter was the same age as Norma. It was only after she had turned eight that Norma had noticed Pierre, the eldest, for the first time. She had been asked to play a tune on the piano at his eighteenth birthday. When she had finished playing, Pierre had gone up to her and kissed her on the right cheek. For a long time afterwards, she had remembered the warmth of that kiss. Whenever she did, her face glowed. She blushed, recalling her nightly ritual, which had since become an automatic gesture.

* * *

Thirty-five years before, Norma's father looked at his wife and his new born infant. His wife could detect the disappointed expression, which he tried to conceal. She knew he had wanted a son to follow in his profession and he had then had to wait three years before this wish was fulfilled when Max had arrived. The family was highly respected in the small town. However, he grew to adore his daughter; Norma was full of laughter with big dark eyes. She followed him around and spent many long hours playing in his study. He was delighted that she was doing excellently at playing the piano. He was full of pride when she played at the school concerts. She was the star at such events, prompting him to say she would become a great concert pianist.

Much to the joy of both parents, Norma passed every music exam with distinction and at the age of eighteen won a scholarship to study in London. Her family contacted Pierre, who was living there, and asked him to make sure she arrived safely and settled into the college halls. He turned up at Victoria Station with his English wife, Rosie, a beautiful, blonde woman.

Pierre greeted her with, "Wow! You have grown up into a pretty girl!"

He introduced Norma to Rosie, who also hugged her and made her feel very welcome. She vaguely recalled his parents not being too pleased with his choice of a wife. After they had lunch, they accompanied Norma to her college halls and made sure she was well settled. Pierre infrequently phoned her during that first year and she stayed with the couple a few times for a weekend in their tiny, one-bedroom flat. They made a bed up for her in their lounge, which was not very comfortable, but she always looked forward to spending time away from halls and its boring food. Rosie was very good to her and she became quite fond of her.

When Norma graduated, her parents had high expectations, but she ended up working as a piano teacher. She also gave private lessons to some of the children in an affluent neighbouring suburb. Her star pupil was young Robbie, who was talented and loved playing the piano, while Judy, Robbie's older sister, was not keen and was hard work. Still, she loved them both and the family often invited her to stay.

Whenever Norma had weekends off, she would meet her few friends from college and some that she had met through Ella. She occasionally stayed at Ella's house and Ella's family always welcomed her. Their respective families regularly visited Ireland and met often in France. Both sets of parents were disappointed that their daughters had not become the concert pianists they had so desired. Norma's parents never visited her in London, although they had promised to. This distressed her as she felt it was their way of letting her know of their disappointment. During past summers, she had made her annual trip to France where she met them at their rented villa. That had stopped some time ago. Like Pierre, his sister and brother had left home and lived in different parts of the world.

Norma dutifully visited her parents in Ireland but was never happy to be there. Her mother was disappointed that she had not yet found a suitable husband and her nagging about being unmarried at this age felt quite tiresome. She continually worried that Norma would end up as a spinster and tried to introduce eligible young men to her. However, Norma thought that most of them were uninteresting and they bored her. She led a very different, progressive lifestyle in England and had very little in common with them.

At the wedding, Pierre took her firmly by the waist and directed her towards the terrace. He offered her a chair and placed another adjacent to hers. He sat down and then stood up, saying, "Back soon! Stay there!" Norma felt puzzled, excited, uncertain and a little insecure. Where had he gone to? Eventually, he returned with two glasses of red wine and a plate of canapés.

Seating himself, Pierre asked, "So, tell me what you've been doing all these years? I don't know why we lost contact. I think it was after you moved south. Are you still there?"

She nodded and gave him a brief account, adding with a laugh, "Robbie is still my star pupil. His parents arranged for him to go to a special school for gifted musical children. He has made excellent progress, but I despair of Judy. She cannot help it. I wish her parents would understand. They keep hoping she will change and dramatically love to play the piano. All she can think about is which parties she has been invited to and what she is going to wear. Anyway, I didn't see you at the church and how did I miss seeing you at the reception? I looked all around. The chap next to me was such a bore!" Then, suddenly she stopped and said, "Where is Rosie? How is she?"

Pierre suddenly looked serious and replied, "I just arrived and, looking around, spotted you. At first, I thought it was my imagination and hesitantly walked closer, before I realised I was right. You look really well." He paused and then continued, hesitantly, "Rosie and I have been divorced for almost five years. She went back to her hometown and I lost all track of her. There was nothing to keep the contact going. We had no children." He waved away her sympathetic acknowledgement, before adding, "We both realised it was a big mistake not long after we had married."

Pierre gulped down his wine and stood up, saying he was going to get another. Soon after, he returned with a bottle and a plate of food. The pair sat there for a long time, exchanging anecdotes and details about their past.

After the wedding, Pierre and Norma met regularly and their relationship grew. She stayed in his spacious flat in an affluent part of London whenever she could. Pierre was running a successful business. One weekend, he divulged that just before he had reconnected with her, he had bought a cottage in a beautiful village up north, which he had just finished decorating. He was expanding his business by opening a branch in a town nearby. His deputy would run the London branch, while he needed to be at the new place to see that the business there ran smoothly. Commuting daily would be tiring, so he had decided to buy a cottage. He asked her if she would accompany him the following weekend, as he had to make sure that all the renovation work had been carried out. He intended to stay there for a while from the beginning of the month.

The cottage was idyllic and Norma immediately fell in love with it. Pierre said he was keeping the London flat. As he talked, Pierre walked to the fridge, grabbed a bottle of champagne and uncorked it. He filled two glasses and placed them on the coffee table near the sofa. This was not unusual as they often drank champagne during the weekends at his flat. Then, kneeling in front of her, he announced, "I would like this to be a double celebration."

Norma looked puzzled.

"Firstly, will you marry me? I think it is time we married. Secondly, to our life together in this dream cottage."

Overwhelmed, Norma cried with joy and nodded. Pierre took out a beautiful solitaire ring from his pocket and placed it on her finger. All she could do was cry. He wiped the tears away and kissed her tenderly. They hugged each other for some time, both feeling they had, at last, reached their destination.

Pierre eventually broke the silence by saying, "When you were eight, I was too old for you, but now you are old enough for me. The ten-year age disparity no longer matters."

Eyes full of love, Norma told Pierre that perhaps that was when she had first fallen in love with him. Playing for him on his birthday had always remained vividly in her mind. She did not tell him about the associated warm feeling on her right cheek that had remained with her to this day or her nightly ritual. Perhaps she had never married anyone else because she had always compared them to him. Now, her simple ritual had meaning, whereas previously she had never understood why such a stupid, trivial action comforted her. It seemed he had always been with her.

"What is that secretive smile about?" Pierre asked, teasingly.

"I'll tell you another day," she replied, the smile widening.

They married two months later and moved into their idyllic cottage, which was the middle one of three. On one side, their retired neighbours used their cottage as a holiday home. They spent most of their time abroad with their children but liked coming back during the summer. A local man came in regularly to maintain the place. Their other neighbour was a young woman, Sarah, who was in her thirties and had a very pretty daughter called Debbie, who was about two and a half. Sarah kept mostly to herself. The rare times they met, she was always polite. She cleaned the small church and vicarage and helped with lunch at the local pub, returning at about four o'clock. Norma concentrated on making the cottage comfortable and spent hours playing the piano. Some days, she met Pierre at the pub for lunch. Sarah was always friendly, but they never saw little Debbie while they were there.

The weather was beautiful that spring and Norma often spent time tending the garden. She noticed that some of the fence panels had collapsed, leaving gaps between their garden and that of Sarah's cottage. She did not think there was any urgency to replace the missing panels. One afternoon, a little head peered through the gap, smiled sweetly and hesitantly walked towards her.

Sarah called out, "What are you doing, Debbie? Come back."

The child hesitated and looked at Norma, who smiled and responded, "It's OK. She can play here if she wants." And that marked the beginning of Debbie's visits. Sarah seemed to have mixed feelings of not wanting to impose on Norma, but relieved to have some time without having to constantly watch the child. From then on, Debbie was a regular visitor and occasionally stayed with Norma in the morning, while her mother was at work. Norma never verbalised her thoughts, but she sometimes missed Judy and Robbie, who now as teenagers were no longer her pupils.

Pierre, who also loved Debbie, saw how engrossed Norma was with her and teased her, "Don't squander all your love on her or you'll have no room for little Pierre when he arrives."

They both laughed. Norma hugged Debbie, playfully responding with, "You'll always be my firstborn." Then, turning to Pierre, she added that they must collect that lovely rocking horse they had bought for Debbie's third birthday.

Autumn came with some fierce windy weather. One morning, Sarah came with Debbie and asked Norma if she could leave her for a couple of hours. She would be back after she had cleaned the church, as she was not going to work at the pub that day. As usual, Norma was willing. Norma thought that Sarah had looked a bit preoccupied recently and was not altogether herself that morning. When Norma had once asked if she was feeling alright, she had quickly smiled, said that she was fine and declined the cup of tea offered.

As usual, Debbie played with her toys and games and loved the piano, tapping away, which was always her special treat. It was nearing lunchtime and Sarah had not returned. Norma gave the child some lunch and they ate together, when Debbie suddenly looked up from her plate and said, "Mummy gone." Norma thought the child was simply stating that her mother was not around. Perhaps she was missing her and was aware that she was late. Norma had a nagging feeling. Had her mother hinted or said something to the child? It was now almost four hours and Sarah had said she would only be away for a couple of hours. Norma felt uneasy and Debbie's remark worried her even more. Her imagination started to play havoc. What had Debbie been told? Was Sarah going away for the night and too afraid to ask if she would take care of the child? Sarah knew how fond she and Pierre were of the child and that they would love to have her stay. Sarah, perhaps, was too afraid to ask and decided not to tell the truth.

An hour later, Norma felt very anxious and started to worry. Eventually, very worried, she phoned Pierre, who told her he would contact Tom at the pub and ring her back. Perhaps Sarah had changed her mind and had gone there after all. Pierre did not phone and Norma intuitively felt that something was not right. Not long after, she saw his car come into the driveway and felt certain he had bad news. Her hunch was right.

16

As Pierre walked in, he lifted Debbie and held her tightly. Leading Norma to the sofa, he sat next to her. Holding Debbie with one arm, he placed the other around her. He stammered, "Very bad news! Very bad news! Sarah was knocked down by a truck." They clung to each other with the child between them. After several minutes of silence, Pierre explained that Sarah had been hit by a truck. She was seriously injured and had been taken to the nearby hospital. The truck driver was unhurt but suffering from shock. Apparently, he had kept repeating, "I could not avoid it. She walked right in front of me. She looked dazed." They remained together until Debbie started to wriggle. Norma took the little girl onto her lap, kissed her and placed her on the sofa next to Pierre. She hardly knew what she was doing. They silently looked at each other and eventually decided to speak to Tom, who informed them that he was coming with his wife and the vicar.

It was unanimously agreed that Debbie would stay with Pierre and Norma for the present. She was fond of them and they were like parents to her. Sarah died on the stretcher as she was being wheeled into the hospital. The impact with the truck had thrown her with such force that almost every bone had been smashed and her organs were severely damaged. If she had miraculously survived, she would have been permanently crippled. The vicar, who had hardly said anything, said that he would make the necessary arrangements with the local funeral furnisher and left.

Pierre broke the long silence that followed the vicar's departure and voiced his thoughts about contacting Debbie's father. Tom shook his head, saying, "That is a mystery. Sarah has never mentioned him and has always been secretive on the subject. She had once said that Debbie was her only family. Her parents split up when she was very little. They lost all trace of her father and believed he emigrated. Her mother died when she was seventeen and she has fended for herself ever since. She never mentioned any other family connections nor divulged who Debbie's father was. When I once tentatively remarked about how proud her father must be to have such a pretty little girl, she just smiled."

His wife gave a little smirk and Pierre picked this up, saying, "Perhaps you know who he is?"

She smiled again and said, "Doesn't she remind you of somebody we all know?"

Tom fidgeted and there was a long silence until Norma burst out, "The vicar!"

They looked at each other and Debbie started to cry. Norma quickly picked her up and tried to soothe her.

Tom eventually said, "Perhaps I should not say this, but now that you have guessed this much… well, we also suspect that she was pregnant again. Recently, she was not very keen on handling the food. One of the staff heard her being sick in the toilet. She quite suddenly appeared in the village, not long after our new vicar came to take the post. Why he did not marry her, we will never know. How she managed to pay for the cottage and meet with expenses has always been a mystery. Her earnings from cleaning and waitressing could not have been enough to pay for it unless she had money of her own. It wasn't long before gossip started to circulate about our young neighbour. Perhaps it was why she kept to herself. There was one thing, though, she loved Debbie. I wonder what is going to happen to her now. The vicar is in his mid-fifties and isn't going to play daddy."

A long silence prevailed before Norma, looking at Pierre, said, "She will stay with us for as long as it is necesary. We will help take care of her until they find a home for her."

Pierre nodded and picked up Debbie, holding her tightly. Tom and his wife left, saying that they were sure the vicar would come and make appropriate arrangements as part of his duty, adding that Debbie was lucky to have such loving people to care for her. Before they left, they helped Norma to bring in Debbie's cot and some clothes and toys, as Sarah had always left her back door unlocked during the day.

The following day, the vicar came to see how Debbie was and promised to make the appropriate arrangements with the local lawyer about her future. He could not thank them enough for continuing to take care of her. He informed them that the lawyer had already begun searching for relatives and looking into temporary care for Debbie until she was adopted. Appropriate funeral arrangements were also being made.

Norma and Pierre spent most of the night thinking about the unexpected revelations. They mutually agreed that they would adopt Debbie unless some relative or other person appeared to claim her. Both silently wished that nothing would obstruct their plan.

* * *

Norma, at ninety-one, was very frail but resilient, of sound mind and verbally eloquent. There was a kind of determination under her dreamy look. She spoke softly, thanking me for agreeing to see her.

After a lengthy pause, she said, "For some time now, I have been using the living room as my bedroom. Both Debbie and Adam realised that I was always obstinate and would not go back to sleep in the bedroom after Pierre died. They rearranged the furniture and as I had a shower room downstairs, I stopped going upstairs altogether. My helper made sure anything I needed was at hand. She has been with me since before Pierre died, eight years ago. Life has never been the same without him. I used to sleep a little, but now I can't. I make myself a pot of tea, which often goes cold. So, I empty the pot and make a fresh one. My doctor gave me some strong sleeping tablets, which I don't take. She knows that and that is why she told me to see you."

During the next few sessions she spoke about her two children, Debbie and Adam and their respective families. She was very fortunate in having such a good family as they were very caring and worried about her. She personally felt she was being a nuisance to them. It was obvious to me that she was troubled by some thoughts that kept her awake at night but refrained from bringing this up. She came on time and, much to my amazement, discovered that she travelled on the underground to come to see me.

Eventually after getting to know her story, she divulged, "I don't know where to begin. As you have probably guessed, the lawyer contacted us, knowing of our wish to adopt Debbie. In due course, he came around with the documents. We were so delighted that we did not stop to look at the documents. It was only a few days later, when we looked more carefully at the papers, that we realised we had been given a birth certificate naming us as Debbie's biological parents." Norma paused, before emphasising, "She was legally our daughter. Pierre said that there was no need to question this and we should accept the documents as they were. After all, what did it matter? We loved her very much, perhaps more so than her own parents had done. We agreed that we would tell her the truth the day after her sixteenth birthday."

After a longish pause she continued, "Debbie, after persistently asking for her mother, soon settled down. By the next spring, much to our delight and joy, I became pregnant. Pierre decided we would move back to London and buy a house with a big garden, which we did. He couldn't bear thinking of me going through the pregnancy in that village. We kept the cottage as a holiday place for many years. Adam and Debbie loved going there, but lost interest as teenagers. Some of our friends used the place in the summer, but it remained vacant for long periods. Eventually, we sold it. Perhaps the memories of that time haunted us."

At the following meeting she related, "Pierre and I never told Debbie as we intended to. We decided to leave it until she was twenty-one. You can guess. We never told her. Before Pierre died, he said that she was so happy now with her family, so why spoil it all? I still feel what we did was not right. She needed to know whether her father was still alive. I know what he did was dreadful. Even though he was in his fifties, he could have done the right thing by Sarah or legally taken over the care of Debbie. We never saw him after the adoption because he was soon transferred to another parish. All this weighs on my mind, especially as Debbie has just become a grandmother. Adam and his wife are already grandparents. They married soon after university in their early twenties, where they met. We thought it was too early for him to settle down, but I now realise that Adam is just like his father. He is a loving, kind and generous person. Both children turned out to be real treasures. I have two great grandchildren."

Although no tears were evident Norma kept mopping her eyes. "We lied. The vicar lied. The lawyer lied. Poor Sarah! When I am awake during the night, I think about her and the awful death she had. How could I tell Debbie about that? That day comes back to me as if it is happening now. When I used to bring it up with Pierre he used to place his arms around me and say, 'Now, where is that warm cheek? Let me give it another kiss to warm it a little more. Just a little one, as I must save some for tomorrow.' I miss him so much and wish I could soon join him. All these thoughts go over and over in my mind." Once more, she dabbed her almost dry eyes.

Norma understood that she could not change the past and eventually decided that she and Pierre had given Debbie a whole lifetime and all the love they could. It was too late to expose the past and create unhappiness to several people. As Pierre had reminded her whenever she spoke to him about Debbie's past, it would not only be distressing to her but to her husband and their children. Perhaps it was best to leave things as they were because what good would it do now? She loved Adam very much, but there was something special about her first experiences with Debbie.

At our penultimate meeting, she said, "At least it is not a secret any more. You now know about it. We lived a lie, but it was because we love Debbie dearly."

Three months later, a brief handwritten note arrived from her doctor to say that she had died in her sleep and that he thought she had felt a lot better after talking to me.

The Walnut Trees

Christmas, as usual, was great. The boys were delighted with their presents and were looking forward to going skiing and meeting some regular acquaintances there, who, like them, went year after year. Anna and Ted watched the boys from the kitchen window, kicking a ball or running around the walnut trees. The trees were bare now, but it had been a good harvest and their friends had received their usual walnuts as Christmas presents. Ted laughingly remarked that neither of the boys would become great footballers while putting his arm around Anna.

Anna said, "They need the fresh air. Let them be out there. I know it won't be long before they come running in saying they're starving, as usual. Perhaps they can come with us this afternoon when we go to the farm to pick up the milk. I'll go and sort out their bags while they're out of the way."

She went upstairs to the boys' bedroom, which was as untidy as ever, carefully stepping between unfinished jigsaw puzzles, cars, books and other toys, while Ted continued to dry and put away the dishes. There were a lot of dishes, including those from last night's dinner. He thought how lucky he was to have a lovely, loving wife and an excellent mother to the boys. Eddie would soon be ten, entering the double figure stage, and Jamie, who was three years younger, had a long way to reach that age.

After stowing away the last saucepan, Ted joined Anna upstairs. Packing for a skiing holiday was a bit of a nightmare. Everything was so bulky or heavy. Once all was packed, except for the last few items, the boys came in, looking for snacks before lunch. Anna had a sore throat and hoped it was not going to get worse. By the evening, her throat had become very sore. She had started coughing and had a temperature.

She had had an awful night and felt really ill. Ted drove her to the nearest town to see the local doctor, who diagnosed it as a virus that was going around, prescribed some antibiotics, and recommended she kept warm and stayed in bed. He said it was doubtful that she would be able to go skiing the following day and that he did not think it was a good idea. Ted thought that they should cancel the trip, but she dissuaded him from doing so. The boys would be disappointed and when she felt better, hopefully in a day or two, she would join them by taking the bus.

"You must be joking! Three bumpy buses! Even if you catch all the connections, it will still take about six hours. No way."

After much persuasion from Anna that they should go as planned, Ted and the boys left later that morning. The boys were quiet at first and felt uneasy about leaving their mother, but as they reached the resort they could not control their excitement. Anna, although she missed them immensely, enjoyed the peace and quiet and all she wanted to do was to stay in bed. She slept poorly, intermittently waking up drenched in sweat. Ted had asked Celine, who usually helped with the cleaning, to come in daily to check that Anna was alright and to make sure she ate properly. He knew how Anna would settle for some fruit and cheese instead of a decent meal.

* * *

Anna, at seventy-six, was still a very attractive woman. She was smartly dressed in a pale grey trouser suit and an immaculate white blouse. She took off her jacket, sat down and took a sip of water from a large bottle. Placing it on the floor next to her, she looked around the room aimlessly and eventually directed her gaze at me. Then, smiling and confidently, she said: "It cools me down and keeps my headaches under control. I never go out without my big bottle of water. My children and some of my close friends tease me, calling it my feeding bottle."

Her GP had referred her because of her severe bouts of headaches, which could not be medically accounted for. Various tests showed no abnormalities. They had started about four years ago, irregularly at first and then almost daily. It was a miracle if she woke up without one. For several weeks, she had spoken incessantly about the preparations for her Golden Wedding Anniversary. The celebration was to include Ted's eightieth birthday, which was a month earlier. Francine, their daughter, was making all the arrangements. She was Ted's favourite and, as a child, he had teased her that she was a throwback with her ruddy, curly hair as he stroked it. Originally, Francine was keen that the celebration should take place in France, where they all loved spending time. However, since the headaches had started, Anna had not been happy about it. Ted also found it too much to travel since his heart attack, preferring to stay at home. Anna refused to go to France and, of course, there could be no celebration without her or Ted. By now, Francine knew how stubborn her mother could be. She had no choice but to agree. She eventually arranged with a nearby restaurant that had special catering amenities for large private parties.

Anna's headaches had started around four years ago, after an evening when she and Ted had gone to visit a couple they had met at a birthday party. The two couples had had much in common and the evening ended with an invitation to come to dinner. It was a beautiful summer's day and they set out earlier than necessary, hoping to go to some of the antique shops the village was noted for, before going on to their friends' house.

Their host had set out a table with drinks near the imitation pond in an immaculately laid-out garden. The fish seemed extra golden, darting around happily, and the flowerbeds with well-thought-out colour schemes looked extraordinarily bright in the sunshine. Anna adored the dark purple, pink and white petunias, which were beautifully and effectively arranged. With much pride, the husband said that his wife managed the garden with the help of a gardener, who came in weekly. He proudly announced that she was born to be creative, placing an arm around her waist and looking at her lovingly. They felt relaxed and really enjoyed the delightful evening. Much later, their host suggested a walk around the wilder part of the garden, while his wife went in to see to the final touches before dinner. While the group wondered around admiring the beautiful plants and shrubs, they came to some very large trees near the back fence. Their host proudly pointed out an almond tree and as he was about to point out the next one, Anna screeched, "A walnut tree!"

24

* * *

"I felt so happy, although I was reminded of our old house and huge garden. I used to spend hours in the garden, not that it was as big as theirs. After Ted's heart attack, we decided to move into a flat with a balcony. It is spacious but not the same."

Looking nostalgic, Anna automatically stretched out for her bottle of water. She went on to explain that by the time they returned to the house, she had a terrible headache and went directly to bed. From then on the headaches started. At first, infrequently and then daily.

Anna looked preoccupied, nostalgic, sighed and drank lots of water from her bottle. This had gone on for many months. She evasively filled her sessions, speaking about her children and the excitement about the Golden Wedding Anniversary celebrations. I often thought about her excessive consumption of water and decided to say what I felt. Intuitively I realised that the walnut tree was of some significance and the excessive drinking of water was connected. I wondered what she was trying to wash away and verbalised my thoughts.

"I wonder what you are trying to wash away since the evening with your friends. It seems as if seeing the walnut tree brought on the headaches in the first place."

She looked at me keenly and I could see her distressed expression. She then looked down and started to play with her hands, twisting, entwining and rubbing them together. A long silence prevailed while she seemed to be struggling with some painful feelings.

Eventually, Anna looked up with a distorted expression and whispered, "Ted keeps saying that I never forgave the children for chopping the trees down to make room for the swimming pool. The walnut tree brought back some memories of those in France I loved so much. The more I think about them the more my head aches."

She remained silent for some time and looked as if in deep thought. I broke the silence to say that seeing the one in her friends' garden stirred up some memories.

After a long pause, she volunteered, "I am not looking forward to the grand Golden Wedding Anniversary party." This was followed by another long silence and while looking at me surreptitiously a few times, she suddenly plonked the bottle she was sipping from on the floor. She rubbed her hands together as if washing them. I noticed a strange, distorted expression and hysterically she burst out, "Francine is not Ted's daughter. To see her making such a fuss only makes me feel worse."

She slumped and swayed forwards and backwards. She cried loudly. After a while she calmed down and said softly, "I feel even more guilty that it is Francine who is making all the effort. She loves Ted so much and he just adores her."

Another long silence prevailed before she related her story.

"Going skiing for the New Year was an annual event we all looked forward to and enjoyed. The year I fell ill, I was distressed not to be going. At first, I wallowed in self-pity, but then I started to enjoy the peace and quiet. There were no hungry boys demanding to be fed, but at the same time I missed them. Ted had always been very supportive and helpful. He was my first and only love. We were a happy family. I read almost everything available and wondered if I should surprise the family by joining them. This was not going to be possible. As it was the holiday period, the buses were not running regularly. It would have been madness to attempt to reach the resort. It was New Year's Eve and that morning I went for a long walk. It was reasonably warm and as I walked past the farm, I noticed that preparations were being made for the barbecue. It was an annual event when a whole pig was roasted on the spit with a roaring fire at another end. All the neighbours come to the party and everyone looked forward to seeing in the New Year together. A few years back, when there was not enough snow to go skiing, we stayed in our cottage and went to the party. We had a really good time. It was a great evening. Everyone was drunk by midnight.

"By the late evening, feeling bored and lonely, I debated whether to go to the party or not. Perhaps going for a short while would do me some good. I was really missing Ted and the boys and felt lonely. I did not want to see the New Year in by myself. The thought depressed me. I could stay indoors, but the change of scene would do me good. Dressing up warmly, I left the house. Louis and Amelia were delighted to see me and that I was feeling a lot better. As Louis poured out a drink for me, a young man came in and Louis introduced me to the stranger. He went on to explain that the man, who was French, was visiting the neighbourhood. They had met at the local bar that afternoon and he had invited him.

"I felt strangely attracted to this man whose name was Andre. I soon realised that the attraction was mutual. We seemed to want to stay with each other the whole evening, although not much conversation of any relevance took place. He didn't speak English and my French was just about passable. There was some wild dancing and once when we laughingly attempted to dance properly, we nearly tripped over. We were often bumped into. Still, it was good fun. After the midnight celebratory glass of champagne, I decided to go home. Andre said he was walking my way and would see me home. It seemed natural when he followed me in and we ended up opening a bottle of champagne. Realising the situation between us was becoming tense, I invited him to look at my walnut trees. I realised that if we stayed indoors I would not be able to resist him. However, my feelings overcame any logical thinking. We ended up making passionate love under one of the walnut trees. What I had tried to avoid happening indoors did, after all, take place. Eventually, we went indoors silently, holding hands, and he stayed the night. He was a passionate man and we repeatedly made love."

After another long pause, looking at her entwined hands on her lap, Anna continued, "I had never experienced such intimacy before. Ted was the only person I had been intimate with and I had always loved Ted. Going with anyone else had never previously crossed my mind, but I found myself experiencing feelings I had not before imagined. The next morning, half asleep, I felt a kiss on my lips and, in a daze, feeling disoriented, I opened my eyes and the events of the previous evening came flooding back. I felt confused, but suddenly noticed that Andre was dressed and ready to leave. Before I could say anything, he embraced me with a passionate hug. I wanted him to make love to me again. Instead, he gently but firmly disentangled himself, blew me a kiss and left."

Anna took a long drink from her bottle and, looking embarrassed, continued her story. That evening she had waited, thinking he would return but he did not. She lay awake for most of the night, confused, willing him to come, feeling guilty and angry with him. Simultaneously, she was shocked at what she had done, reminding herself that she loved Ted. It was all a big mistake and she must get Andre out of her mind. Yet the thought of his body, smell, smile – kept coming back. She dressed early the next morning and went for her usual walk. She was tempted to go and chat with Amelia, hoping to hear something about Andre, but changed her mind. She never saw or heard from him again. A few days later, she made some furtive enquiries without trying to give away the confusion, anger, pain and longing she felt. Louis related that he had met him at the bar and had spontaneously invited him to come. He had not a clue as to where he was staying or where he had come from. Perhaps he was passing through. No one knew him or saw him again. He vanished as mysteriously as he had appeared.

By late February, she realised she was pregnant. Both she and Ted were sometimes careless and did not take the necessary precautions. A nagging feeling told her it was not Ted's child. When the baby arrived, they were delighted to have a daughter. It was Ted's idea that she should be called Francine, because she was the magic baby they had conceived in France. As Francine grew up, her mop of tawny, ruddy curls, dark eyes and smile continuously haunted Anna. Whenever Ted was his generous and kind self, her guilty feelings were agonising. There were times she felt she should confess the truth, but when she realised the pain and aftermath, she stopped herself from doing so. What good can come from such a confession? Ted's aunt had once said that there was a great aunt who had dark red hair, but Anna remained quiet and did not respond. She once jokingly said to one of her close friends, who admiringly referred to how attractive Francine was becoming, that it was because she was her lover's daughter. The friend laughed and that was the closest she had ever been to confessing her secret.

Francine followed Ted around and she was his 'little pet'. He could not do enough for her. Each time they went to France, she both wished and dreaded that she might meet Andre, but she never saw him again. Sometimes, she hoped and longed she would, but quickly gathered her straying thoughts together. As a child, Francine reminded her of Andre, but as time passed and she moved out, married and had three beautiful children of her own, the memory faded away. At Ted's seventieth birthday party, all three children made speeches. Francine's was most touching and seeing her husband and daughter together stirred up some feelings Anna had shelved away.

Soon after that she had dreams in which Andre appeared. The dinner party and the walnut tree opened the floodgates and the migraine started. Ted explained the migraine as not being able to accept that the children had chopped down her favourite trees to make room for the swimming pool. She felt very tempted to confess the truth about her love affair under those walnut trees and the real reason as to why they were so significant to her. But how could she be so cruel to someone who had been so wonderfully kind and generous to her? Ted already had heart problems. It would be the death of him. And what would it do to Francine? The whole family would suffer. It had to remain with Anna until she went to her grave, but since the dinner party, the headaches had refused to go away.

At the age of seventy-six, Anna was beginning to share those secrets. When Ted made tentative enquiries about her meetings with me, she lied to him. To make him feel good she told him it was to do with the chopping down of her favourite walnut trees and perhaps missing the house and garden they had. Maybe she was also missing their old house and garden and becoming envious when she saw their friends' house and garden. He roared with laughter and said that he had already told her about the chopping down of the walnut trees. If she paid him all the money she was spending on these sessions, they would be so much richer. It took many more months before she could come to terms with her long-standing secret.

Continuing she said, "I know it was terrible of me to deceive such a loving husband and father. I blame what I did on the champagne, but I also know that is no excuse. Sometimes, I think the lies are worse than what I did. But how can I ruin the happiness and the loving relationship between Francine and Ted. Perhaps she would not have had that with Andre. I sometimes wonder if he had a wife and a family of his own. We never shared any personal details. At times, it felt like it was all a very pleasant dream, but at other times the nightmares perished those thoughts and the headaches returned with a vengeance."

Nearing the end of one of her therapy sessions, Anna remained silent for a long time as if caught up in her own daydream world. She eventually divulged, "I lay awake for a long time last night. I feel a lot better for having spoken to you about all this. The headaches have not gone altogether. They come and go infrequently. I constantly ask to be forgiven for deceiving such a good husband, but how could I directly ask him to forgive me? To tell him now would bring on another heart attack and probably kill him. I suppose I will have to live with my lie now. When I saw the happiness on Ted's face at our Golden Wedding celebration, I realised how lucky I am. Perhaps it was just as well that Andre disappeared. If we met again, I really don't know what would have happened."

There was a long pause before she added, "I do love Ted very much and I worry about his health. I cannot imagine my life without him."

Some thoughts

Both Norma and Anna's stories concern their daughters whom they loved. The dilemma was that they were connected with secrets and lies that had been kept until they were old people. Why had they become distressed and anxious about their secrets at this stage, when they had kept them hidden for so long? Truthfully, I do not have any definitive answers, but perhaps thoughts about the nearness of death and dying made them feel guilty and they felt the need to reassess, confide or expose their secrets. They needed to grieve and come to terms with their deceitful behaviour. However well meant, they knew and felt that their actions were morally wrong. They also realised that they had lived a life of deceit and it was too late to tell the *truth*. Considered from an alternate perspective, the *truth* was that both concealed their secrets with good intentions and, with hindsight, perhaps this was the best choice. Confiding the *truth* at this late stage would only be too painful to the younger women. Discovering the truth would have created a whole range of emotional unrest to them and their families.

In Debbie's case she should have been told when she was in her teens. But with Francine it was different. Too many people would have been hurt. Ted may have forgiven Anna. At this late stage speaking to a non-judgemental listener did not altogether free these women of their irresponsible behaviour, but it helped them to integrate those activities as part of their life experiences. In doing so, Norma and Anna recognised their negative behaviour and felt less burdened. They felt much better for having confided the truth. Consequently, they felt alleviated of some of their distress. Norma felt less distressed and Anna's health improved which enabled her to support Ted during his illness.

In Norma's case, Debbie was given a better life than perhaps she would have had with her own mother, Sarah. The probability was that Sarah, a vulnerable young woman who was coping with one young child and another on the way, already feeling insecure, would not have been able to give Debbie the lifestyle she had with Norma and Pierre. Sarah's childhood had been a disturbed one. She came over as a very needy young woman. There are no certain answers as to why she went on living in the village near the vicar, who was emotionally abusive. Did he, to some extent, replace the father who had deserted her during her childhood? It seems she was prepared to do anything to remain close to the vicar. She must have been in a delicate, unbalanced, emotional state to have done what she did. The vicar's behaviour was, without doubt, scandalous and these days may have been exposed through the media. Debbie was very fortunate to be taken on by Pierre and Norma. They gave her so much love and a comfortable home.

Similarly, Francine was loved more by Ted than she may have been by Andre. Anna concluded that Andre was irresponsible and unreliable. We will never know how truthful this is, except that Andre's behaviour seemed strange. Anna acknowledged that she had also been irresponsible in giving in to his charms. She felt grateful that he had not returned, because she knew he was nothing like her dear Ted and could not envisage a future with him. She felt certain she would have regretted leaving Ted. We will never know, except for the reality that Francine had a secure base and grew up to respect and love Ted dearly.

With both Norma and Anna, the belief that as one gets older one recalls and remembers earlier times with more clarity is true. Irrepressible misdemeanours from the past have to be revisited and renegotiated with 'new eyes' before they can be internally accepted as part of the personality. Perhaps the inevitable preoccupation of feelings and thoughts about death and dying stirs up a need for a reassessment of the past. Guilt obviously played a significant and vital role in wanting to make reparations. After much self-debating and weighing the pros and cons of confessing at this stage, which would disrupt their daughters' lives, the two women decided not to tell them the truth, as this will only create more problems and pain. It was also understood that, at this late stage, it was not only the daughters that would be involved but their spouses and children. Even if their daughters decided to keep the information to themselves, they would be burdened with the secrets, which might eventually cause more pain.

Norma and Anna felt some relief for having shared their secrets, as they were not secrets any longer. They realised that it was part of their inner state they would have to accept. What had been done

----

could not be undone. Sadly, neither Debbie nor Francine would ever get to know their extended family members connected to their fathers, but Norma and Anna consoled themselves with the thought that there were many such people who had lost contact with their relatives. Norma and Anna came over as honest, caring and loving people. Both had given their respective daughters much love and care.

At her final meeting, Anna told me that, "My headaches are not as frequent. I feel a lot better now that I have shared all this with you. I am pleased I did not, after all, tell my husband or Francine. What good would it do either of them?"

I did not make the decision of whether she should tell her husband and daughter the truth. Mine as previously stated is a non-judgemental role as that of a catalyst. With hindsight, I do feel that it was better to not share their secrets than to destroy the happiness of two people and perhaps others as well.

2

BETRAYAL

Rightly or wrongly, there are people who feel they have betrayed loved ones or have been unfairly betrayed themselves. In the first story, a son feels he has betrayed his parents and especially his father. The second story concerns a woman who feels betrayed by her mother and her grandparents. In both scenarios, whatever the circumstances, the behaviour of those concerned reacted negatively on the emotional lives of these two people.

The Lost Father

"We have to go, darling, whether you want to or not – or, at least, you must. I am willing to come and wait at the hotel if you would prefer that. We cannot do the journey in a day. I will book a room at the Crown."

Henry stood in the kitchen, holding the mug of tea he had been handed by Carol. He looked shocked and bewildered. She gently took the mug from him and led him to a chair at the table, which he slumped into. Placing the tea on the table, she pulled a chair opposite his, sat down and took hold of both his hands. They felt icy cold and lifeless. Silently, she rubbed them, as if trying to energise and stir some warmth into them, and patiently waited for him to respond. He remained silent and then the tears slowly started to flow. He sobbed and sobbed uncontrollably and Carol was very worried. She stood up, walked round to him and cradled his head. He continued to sob. She was shocked to see him in this state. He was always so confident and the one who usually took over the responsibility during a crisis. She was trying to be brave, but was very worried. Eventually, she called the doctor.

It seemed hours before he arrived. After listening to Carol, the doctor presumed it was the shock and sedated him, suggesting he needed to rest. He promised to call the next morning when he thought that Henry would feel a lot better. He also said that Carol should not make any travel arrangements until he had seen Henry the next day. He patted her on the shoulder as he left.

While Henry was asleep, Carol phoned Larry, their eldest son, giving him the news about his grandmother and the impact it had had on his father.

Impatiently, Larry replied, "What is all the drama about? Why on earth is he taking it all so tragically? For heaven's sake, she is ninety-two and off her rocker. He always complained of how frail she was and how she probably didn't understand anything he said to her. He couldn't bear to see her so weak and dependent, saying it would be better if she just went. Why is he putting on such an act now?"

Larry ended the conversation by saying he would drop in first thing in the morning. It was no use coming over now as Henry was asleep. Carol had a light supper and went up to pack their suitcase, as it was obvious that she would have to go with Henry. Whatever the doctor said, Henry would want to go as soon as possible. Not knowing how long they might stay, she packed a few extras.

The next day, after getting consent from the doctor that Henry was fit enough to travel, they set off on the long drive. Henry obediently settled in the passenger seat and Carol drove off. For once, Henry did not dispute her decision and sat quietly looking out of the window. Carol was aware that he was still in a stunned state and was not really taking in anything.

When they stopped for lunch, he volunteered, "I hope she stays alive until we get there. I want to hold her hand while it's still warm."

Carol reminded him that none of his siblings had phoned with any further news. Luke, his younger brother, certainly would have done so if anything had happened. Henry grunted and murmured something inaudible. She was both shocked and puzzled at his behaviour. He was always so calm and logical about everything.

When they arrived, Henry remained in his seat, strapped-up. Exhausted, Carol impatiently told him to unstrap the seat belt and get out. Henry seemed preoccupied and unaware of his surroundings. Taking him by the arm and surprised by her tone of voice, Carol gently led him to the building. He walked slowly with his head bowed. Usually, Carol had to half run beside him as he galloped with his long strides.

Luke, who had seen them through the window, appeared from nowhere and hugged them. He gave Carol a puzzled smile and an understanding nod as he noted Henry's unfamiliar behaviour. He led them to the private room he had arranged for his mother. She was obviously still alive. Henry vaguely commented on her being moved. She had previously been in a private care home. He sat on the chair near the bedside and cradled his mother's inert hand, which lay on the bedcover, in both of his and gave a huge sigh. Tears started to roll down his cheeks as he kissed her hand several times. She was surrounded by drips and gadgets. Her face looked distorted and askew, and saliva ran down the side of her mouth. In the half-lit room, she already looked like a corpse stretched out.

Henry, silently weeping, said softly, "'She was always so dignified and beautiful with such refined features. I remember how her long fingers used to move on the keyboard."

Henry kept rubbing her hand or giving it a gentle squeeze as if trying to bring it to life. When he had done this during previous visits, she would give him a sweet, frail smile. Occasionally, she would touch his face. Such thoughts brought on more tears and heaving, and Carol cradled his head to calm him down. Eventually, he did and just sat there, holding his mother's hand.

Luke looked at Carol and silently indicated that they should leave the two alone for a while. As they walked out of the door, a nurse was about to enter. Luke waylaid her to give Henry a few minutes alone with their mother, as well as to question her about the prognosis. She informed him it was just a matter of time now as not only was she severely paralysed, but her heart was very weak. Henry and Luke stayed at her bedside, taking turns to stay in the room. Although Luke did not say anything, he was perturbed by the unexpected change in Henry. It was a shock to see his very confident brother looking so frail, inadequate and depressed. Their mother died in the early hours of that morning, with Henry holding her hand and Luke standing by the bed, looking at them. He could not help thinking that Henry had always been her favourite and a pang of jealousy ran through him.

Henry's story

After the funeral, Henry changed significantly. He restlessly and almost silently wandered around the house and garden. Tears would appear and Carol became quite concerned. The doctor said he was mildly depressed and prescribed antidepressants. He suggested that Carol try to cheer him up by trying to go back to their previous lifestyle of entertaining and having the grandchildren around as much as possible. Although over the months his condition improved slightly he had spurts of feeling very low. He disliked the idea of being on any kind of medication and, fortunately, had previously always enjoyed a healthy lifestyle. He hated taking the antidepressants and a friend suggested he saw a psychologist, which he did. The psychologist realised that there were some long-standing emotional problems and referred him for psychotherapy.

Henry was a slim, very handsome, distinguished-looking man and had an air about him that suggested he was usually in control. I was surprised that he had had a minor breakdown. Although, from my clinical experience, I realised I should know better. Outer physical appearance and the display of looking confident is not always a sign that the person feels secure. Inner turmoil can be well hidden from scrutiny.

As his story unfolded over the months, a sense of his real self became more obvious. Inner conflict, no matter how well hidden, is part of one's personality and is inseparable from who one is. Those images, when irrepressible, veer their ugly heads when least expected and puzzle others.

Henry's mother had moved to be near Luke and his family after the death of her husband. As the years went by, she moved into sheltered accommodation and then went into a nursing home. She was regularly visited by her two daughters, Luke and Henry. He disclosed how sad it made him feel to watch her grow too frail to do anything for herself, to be bedridden and senile. She had been an active woman. It upset him too much to be with her when she no longer recognised him, but always smiled. He found it painful and at times wished she would die. When he took their dog to be put down, he wished he could do the same for his mother.

"I should have been relieved when she died. She was no more than a vegetable! The funeral was a traditional Christian one, attended by all my family and friends."

Everything Henry disclosed during our early meetings seemed normal, logical and sensible. He attended regularly and talked about his daily life, which would be the envy of most people. However, I could not help feeling that there was some undercurrent activity that he was reluctant to talk about or something gnawing internally that was frustrating him. Why the breakdown? After several sessions of relating light, peripheral anecdotes, I suggested that perhaps there were two Henrys – one that tried to be his usual confident self and the other, silent one, who had negative feelings lurking around and a mind full of unspoken thoughts. Perhaps he was silently trying to understand them.

Henry was constantly searching for answers for his unhappy feelings. He looked at me keenly and remained silent. Following that meeting, he started to talk about some of his earlier life and background over several weeks, which initially did not seem to be of much significance. He often looked uncomfortable and hesitant, as if he did not want to disclose what was troubling him. Over six months of meeting regularly, I suggested that perhaps he no longer needed to see me.

Henry smiled and replied, "But I like coming. This is a time when I can say things I never talk about with others, like talking to you about how proud I am of my sixteen-year-old grandson being chosen as the captain of the cricket team. He reminds me of myself. I would not say that to anyone else. Not even to my wife. She would only laugh and say I am being pompous."

"What is it about your grandson that reminds you of yourself?"

"I was also good at sports. I was an all-rounder."

Henry looked a bit bashful and smiled. With some encouragement, this small revelation led to an insight into his very disturbed adolescent years. His ancestry went back to the north of England where the coal mining industry had flourished during his childhood and adolescence. His grandfather, who had been a miner, broke tradition by refusing to let his son, Henry's father, go down into the mines. Instead, he arranged for him to be apprenticed as a lift engineer – a job he held for many years. Henry's father, who was a very handsome man, married into a middle-class family against the wishes of Henry's mother's parents. They continued to live in the same district, although his maternal relations refused to have anything to do with his father.

"My mother usually took me with my two younger sisters and brother to visit them. When I was about fourteen, I realised that my grandmother never stopped criticising my mother. She never forgave her for marrying beneath her social background. I also noted that my granddad was too afraid to contradict his wife or even say anything at all. He was very fond of my mother. My grandmother was a real tartar. Without fail, they never forgot our birthdays or presents on Christmas Eve, but my father never came with us on these visits. Once, I asked my mother why they never came to visit us like my father's parents. She evaded my question by saying something like they were too set in their old ways. My paternal grandparents usually spent Christmas Day with us, but I never took to them. That grandmother was the opposite of the other. She was always so loud and as I grew up, I thought her vulgar. But from very early on, I sensed the strained atmosphere between my mother's parents and my father. Visiting them was like going to another planet. We were not allowed to run around, be noisy or have fun. I once asked my mother why father did not ever come with us to visit granddad and grandma. I remember her saying that he had a lot of work to do and he could get on with it without being disturbed when he was alone. It was about that time that I learnt the truth. My parents were arguing over something, not realising I was in my room. Then, I heard my father verbally abusing my grandmother."

For the first time, I was learning about Henry's earlier life. After this long spiel, he paused and looked at me intently. I waited. Eventually, he continued, "I was shocked to hear my father call them 'posh hypocrites'. It was then that I discovered that they were totally against my parents' marriage."

Henry's mother was an educated woman, who encouraged him with his schoolwork and taught him to play the piano. He won a scholarship to go to a grammar school and then his father decided to send him to a boarding school to complete his A Levels, "where he would learn to become a real gentleman". After an Oxbridge academic education, he moved to London to work there.

Henry gave a big sigh and kept nodding. I repeated "a real gentleman" and he continued, between pauses, "My father achieved what he wanted. Throughout my adolescence, I felt ashamed of my background and especially my father's link with the mines. My father was very proud of his brainy son and he could not stop showing me off whenever the opportunity arose. I dreaded going home during the holidays. What started as a small lie led to a string of lies. I started to lie about my background. I told my friends that my father was in the Foreign Office and that was the reason for being sent to boarding school. I had once gone on a school trip to France and the idea of having a home somewhere abroad appealed to me. I often managed to be invited somewhere by one of my friends and spent most of my holidays with them."

Henry started to become emotional and the tears started to come. After another long pause, he divulged, "The lies started to come easily. I lied and lied and lied. It is amazing how once I started, it became almost automatic. I told them that my mother was a very good pianist, which to some extent was true, because she was. She taught me and my siblings to play the piano. My youngest sister is pretty good. Slowly but positively, I disconnected with my parents and siblings. My two younger sisters remained in the north and married local men. My youngest brother, Luke, moved to the big city and started a business there. He still runs what has become a very successful business. He seems happily married with a family and a luxurious lifestyle. He is one of the 'nouveau riche' – you know, the brash, pompous kind. They own several cars and give large parties at posh hotels. Carol and I initially went to them, but we had nothing in common with Luke's friends and have made excuses since the children arrived. I very rarely see any of my siblings."

Following this meeting, in which Henry divulged so much of his personal activities and feelings, other long-kept secrets came to the fore. He recalled what he now considered as disreputable and disgusting behaviour towards his father, whom he realised had loved him so much. He would not be who he was without his father encouraging him to get an education and move away from the background he was stuck in. He realised that his father was a very intelligent man, who had not had the opportunities he himself so enjoyed. He saw his maternal grandparents as vain and only interested in materialism. From thereon, he more readily shared his feelings. He wished he had

----

understood his father better and so could have appreciated the person he really was and spent more time with him.

"My father had a minor accident in his late fifties when two of his fingers were jammed in a lift. Luke and I decided he should retire and helped our parents financially. It was about then that the mines were being closed. Not long after, in his early sixties, my father died of a heart attack. I felt like a stranger at his funeral. It was then that my mother moved into a flat to be close to my brother."

Henry sobbed silently, holding his handkerchief close to his mouth.

* * *

A few months later, Henry walked in wearing a dark suit.

"It's Carol's birthday and I'm taking her out to dinner. She has been so understanding and helpful during these last few months. I know I must have been difficult to live with being in a cocoon. I felt that she needed some extra attention this birthday, so I told the family we were going out alone and that the usual family party could wait for another day."

Henry took off his jacket, laid it carefully on a chair and sat down with a sigh. He was at a stage when he now spoke freely about most of his feelings and what he recalled and remembered from the past.

"After graduating, I was apprenticed to a huge law firm in London. I met Carol at a company party and after nearly two years of being together, we decided to have a quiet wedding. My parents and Luke and his wife were the only people from my family who attended. I never got on with my sisters and they made excuses and did not come. I believe they called me 'Mr Posh'. My wife knows very little about them as we rarely see them. The last time we met was at my brother's silver wedding anniversary party. Carol does not know the details about my family history but has accepted that I do not get on with them. My father did not survive for many years after we married. He was ill at the time and looked frail. My mother was her usual serene, calm self, but I knew she liked Carol very much. After our short honeymoon, Carol insisted we travel up north to see them. I saw the faint but warm smile my father often gave Carol and knew he was happy with my choice and to see me being happy."

Henry looked down for some time, silently engrossed in thought. After a short time, he looked up and said, "Thinking back about my father and the way I treated him makes me feel awful. How could I have been so cruel? All he wanted for me was to be well educated and he worked hard to give me that. It was an opportunity he never had. I now realise that he was a very clever man who read and spoke intelligently. He was a perfect match for my mother."

Henry continued to come regularly and revealed much of his secret past life and the lies that he told to maintain it. Once the lying started, he began to believe that he was who he said he was. He felt he had betrayed his parents and especially his father, who had always been proud of him. Much to Henry's embarrassment, his father used to boast to his friends that his son was the star of the village.

Sobbing uncontrollably, he whispered, "How I wish I could speak to my father and tell him how sorry I am. He was a good man and a clever man, who was highly respected by the community. I should be thankful and proud of him. I betrayed him. I am sure my mother guessed my feelings, but she never, ever reprimanded me for behaving the way I did. She was a stoic woman and when she died, I realised it was too late as I would never be able to tell her about my behaviour."

"Carol liked my father and spent time discussing various subjects with him, ones that I never realised my father was knowledgeable about. She never told me if they discussed anything personal, nor questioned me about the strained relationship between my sisters and myself. She comes from a very middle-class, professional background and they never discuss personal details. They keep their emotions very much in control." Laughingly, he added, "Like myself. Who am I to criticise her? Anyway, when my father died, she insisted that we stay with my mother for two weeks and help her to sort out various things. My sisters were not too keen about that, although they were always polite to Carol. She has a way of getting on with people without being intrusive. She is not the type to ask personal questions. She has always been willing to listen to others and anything I wished to speak about. We have been very happy together. She spends much time helping with our grandchildren."

Henry continued to come to see me and mourn the loss of his parents. He decided to confide in his wife and felt that she would be understanding and a good listener. He conveyed that she had already guessed some of his secrets but had never reproached him. Through her persuasion, Henry recently visited Luke and his family and Henry promised to make the effort to get to know his sisters and their families better. Carol suggested that Henry arrange a family reunion on his next birthday.

Some thoughts

By the age of seventy-four, Henry had been very successful in his chosen profession; he had married Carol when they were both in their late twenties and his family now consisted of three children and several grandchildren. He played golf and bridge, was a member of a fitness club and socialised regularly. However, unaware of his mental situation, he remained stuck at the adolescent stage of his life experiences. This is, perhaps, not unusual, as many of us do not grow into well-balanced adults without some childish and adolescent characteristics remaining with us throughout our lifetime. However, with Henry, there was a long-standing, serious denial, which brought about the current minor breakdown.

When the nursing home phoned to say that his mother, who was in her nineties, had had a stroke, his world collapsed. He had last visited her about a month ago, on one of his routine trips. Perhaps he realised that he would now never be able to tell her some of the truth about his feelings. Previously his thoughts were about staying at The Crown, where the manger knew them well. In the summer, the countryside felt relaxing and was beautiful. They enjoyed their long walks there. He said that it was so much more interesting and better than walking on the Heath or in the parks of London. His thoughts evolved around the outer world whilst the inner world was kept well repressed.

While writing about Henry, I wondered how common an experience this really is, because I have heard similar stories when working with adolescents and adults. During adolescence, feelings of independence, together with not liking what parents expect, or who they are, often leads to feeling ashamed or wishing for a different type of parent or parents. Adolescence is also a stage of life that involves unpredictable emotional turbulence. Many reflect on how awful a time it was. Maturing from dependency towards independency may also feel like a time for attaining a new identity. Most people, by adulthood, move to a state of maturity, although pockets of earlier stages of emotional behaviour remain and may reappear during one's adulthood. When the adolescent becomes so involved in his own wishes and targets, they have very little time to consider what their parents or carers are feeling. They swivel around a fictitious world of their own and, at times, it becomes too late to change the past.

Undoubtedly, it was too late for Henry to change the course of what had been because time had moved on and the past could not be changed. The river that has determinedly established a course towards the sea cannot start running backwards to alter its path. It may run off at a tangent or its waters may terminate as a dam. However, it is possible for people to recognise their unrealistic behaviour towards others and make amends. But this was not possible for Henry. His father, who had loved him and was very proud of him, had been long dead. However, the 'dammed up' guilty feelings recalled from memory could no longer be controlled and the banks burst during the time of his mother's death. The shock that came with knowing he would never be given the opportunity to confide his feelings to his father or mother brought about a minor breakdown. It became clear to him that no matter how successful his lifestyle had been, the traumas of childhood and adolescence remained shelved somewhere in his internal world.

From my clinical experience, I have gathered that the psychopathology of those vulnerable times may return with urgency and demand reconciliation during later life. Perhaps growing old is a time when one is confronted with the trials and tribulations of earlier days. For many, growing dependency, degenerative sexuality and other biological changes remind them of earlier times. While feeling frustrated, tormented and, at times, incapacitated, growing old becomes a period of coping with current difficulties. It is also a time of involution. Henry's story is much more common than people are aware of.

The Lost Mother

Tessa danced around the room with the letter held to her bosom. She picked up her violin and swayed around, intermittently showering it with kisses, half shouting and half singing, "I've done it! I've done it!"

Her grandmother, wondering what the commotion was about, walked into the room. Tessa ran up to her and hugged her, her words spilling over each other. She tried to explain the good news while waving the letter. Her grandmother took the letter from her and read it. She gave Tessa a huge hug and said: "You've done it, my baby! Well done!" By now, the tears were running down her cheeks. They eventually calmed down and read the letter, aloud, together.

"We are pleased to offer you a place at the music college… etc…"

Tessa and her grandmother went down to tell her grandfather, who was pottering in the garden. Tessa's grandmother went to put on the kettle to make the inevitable pot of tea to celebrate the good news. From then on, the conversation was about Tessa preparing to leave home in late August to start on her future career as a violinist. She was talented and had worked very hard to achieve her aim. The college was a prestigious one, which had produced many an artist in the musical field.

Tessa was nearly four when her father, Calum, contacted her grandparents telling them they must come and sort out their daughter and take charge of their granddaughter. He was intending to leave as he had had enough. Tessa's grandparents left immediately for Wales. On arrival they found Mildred in a drunken stupor. Calum had gone out with Tessa for a walk to tell her that she will not be seeing him for a while as he had to go away. She will be staying with grandpa and grandma until mummy is better. When he returned he told Mildred's parents that he would have left a long time ago if it had not been for Tessa. As he had no definite plans he felt that Tessa will be better off with them for the present. Mildred was in no state to take care of her. He had arranged for her to go into a clinic for treatment. The neighbours reported that the couple quarrelled frequently. It was mostly about Mildred being drunk. The smell of burnt food in the evenings often angered Calum, who was a hard worker and a good man. He would come home from work hoping to have a decent meal and a quiet evening with his family, but then the rows would start.

Tessa could only really remember growing up with her grandparents and her Uncle Ted. It was soon discovered that she was musically talented when she started playing the violin at primary school, leading to extra tuition from a specialist instructor.

Soon after receiving the acceptance letter from the music school, the euphoria ended, bringing feelings of uncertainty and fear over what might happen. She was leaving home to go to the big city, away from her beloved grandparents and friends. On the day she moved, after her grandparents had left, she experienced a mixture of tears and excitement over what the unknown future held for her. She quickly discovered that she had entered a very competitive world. There were many confident young men and women, who were all very talented and wanted to achieve as much as she did. The standard was very high. Tutors demanded the best. After long hours of practising with her personal tutor, who was unlike her kindly one back at home, she started to feel insecure. Some days, she went back to her room and cried, feeling that she could not go on. She felt lonely, insecure and unhappy. She could not cope with the demands and was almost on the brink of a breakdown.

Towards the end of her first year, as she was walking towards the dining hall for dinner, she met Susan, someone she had become friendly with, dashing out in a hurry, quickly explaining that she was meeting her parents for dinner. Tessa felt a lump in her throat. Gasping, she walked back to her room. She lay on her bed. Her head started to pound as if it was going to split. She took a couple of painkillers which did not help. After a restless night she was sick the next morning and had to stay away from college. For many days afterwards, she was unable to continue with her practising and was persuaded to see a doctor. After examining and listening to her he recognised that she was anxious and over stressed. He prescribed some antidepressants and suggested she stayed away from classes for a week. However, Tessa could hardly continue with her tuition and eventually it was decided by the tutors that she should have the remainder of the academic year off and start afresh the next year.

Feeling too ashamed to tell her grandparents, who were many miles away, she moved in with a friend's friend, who had a small spare room. While still on antidepressants, which made her feel high, she found herself a part-time job at a local supermarket. She phoned her grandmother regularly and went to stay with her grandparents during what would have been college breaks.

They had just finished lunch – which Tessa had hardly eaten and was reprimanded for it – when Tessa, finding it unbearable to contain any longer, burst out, "What really happened to my mum and dad? Where are they now? I would like to meet them."

Her grandmother, shocked at the unexpectedness of the question, almost dropped the plates. She sat down and looked at her husband. He said, "Tell her the truth." Tessa looked from one to the other and after a long pause, shaking her head, her grandmother disclosed, "Your father is alive and living in Canada. That is where we last heard from him. He is a good man. It was all your mother's fault. He contacted us one day saying he had had enough. We must come and fetch the both of you. He was leaving your mum. We brought the both of you back from Wales and placed her at a clinic, but she refused treatment and ran away. We tried our best but could not find her. After the first few months when you used to cry for mummy, you settled down and we never spoke about her to you. Believe me, not a day goes by without me regretting what happened."

Tessa yelled uncontrollably, "Where is she? Where is she? I want to go to her." Grandma burst out crying inconsolably and Tessa put her arms around her. After some time, the elderly lady stopped crying and quietly told Tessa that she had something to confess. The tears started to flow again and Grandpa, who had been standing at the door, said, "Let's go downstairs. I'll put the kettle on and we can tell Tessa everything."

By now, Tessa did not know what she felt. She alternated between feeling confused, angry and curious, while following her grandparents downstairs. They all sat down and quietly waited, each engrossed with their own thoughts until mugs of tea were placed in front of them. Then, Grandma revealed, "Your mum was a very clever person, but unfortunately met a guitarist at university with an alcohol problem. She was then twenty and became infatuated with him and started drinking with him. He led her astray, but then he dropped out and disappeared. She was devastated and that was when the alcohol problem really became serious. All the same, she managed to get her degree and soon after left for Wales perhaps in the hope of finding him. We were pleased when she met your father, Calum. He managed to get her off the alcohol and they married a few months before you arrived. She loved you very much, but the alcohol problem started again when you were just over two. She started to drink secretly, hiding the vodka from your dad. When he realised what was happening, he sent her to a clinic, but she ran away. Believe me, your dad tried so hard to help her, but eventually he found it impossible to cope. He contacted us to fetch you and sort out your mum. He left with the promise that there would be money forwarded through the bank for you. He kept his promise."

She once more burst into tears while Grandpa coaxed her to have her tea, which she had not touched and was now cold. Eventually, she stopped sobbing and continued, "When you were twelve, your dad contacted us to say he would like to come and see you. This was not long after your mother had died."

Tessa stood up and screamed, "My mother died! My mother died!" Both her grandparents held her and tried to calm her. Eventually she calmed down and her grandmother continued.

"She had gone from bad to worse, squatting in various places. She did try to come and see you a few times when you were very young, but she was always drunk. Your Uncle Ted told her that your dad had taken you away and that we had no idea where you were. You were doing well at school and we thought it best to wait until you were older."

Tessa turned and alternately looked from one to the other. She was as white as a sheet. As she stood up, her grandfather came to put his arm around her. She moved away and, without saying a word, rushed upstairs and locked herself in her bedroom. She lay on her bed and stared at the ceiling, feeling quite numb. She felt too shocked and was in a daze. She vaguely heard the knocking on her door and her grandfather's pleas sounded as though they were coming from a distance.

Much later she learnt that her mother was found dead in London and the police broke the news to her grandparents. She had carried their address in a little purse they found amongst her belongings. She had been squatting in an old building with some other alcoholics.

Tessa's story

All of this was related intermittently between sobbing and long pauses. After nearly nine months of regular meetings, Tessa decided she was going to do two things. Firstly, she was going to visit her mother's grave. Secondly, she was going to try and trace her father through the bank. She discovered that he was still sending her a monthly allowance which her grandparents at first spent on her tuition fees and later gave it to her as pocket money. Much to her distress, she discovered that her mother was cremated as Uncle Ted thought that was the best solution. However, she successfully contacted her father who was just as pleased to hear from her. He arranged for her to visit him in Canada where she spent three weeks with him, her stepmother, stepbrother and stepsister. She related that she felt completely at home with them and could not wish for a better father. He never hesitated to answer her questions about her mother and had a large envelope of photos of all three of them. She realised she had many of her mother's features.

She slowly came to terms with what her grandparents had done. It seemed that her grandmother had been the stronger willed and her grandfather had given into her scheme of thinking. When she had first asked about her parents, she was told that they had died in a car accident while travelling abroad. They said her parents had left her with them as she was too young to go. It was the reason they had stopped her father from coming to see her when she was twelve.

During her analysis, Tessa had gone back to college to continue with her career as a violinist. At first, it was a state of uncertainty and fear. She discovered from her father that his mother had been a very good pianist, although she did not train professionally as one. She probably inherited her musical talent from her. With his encouragement, she persevered and qualified as an accomplished violinist. The highlight of her attainment was when her father and stepfamily came to the graduation ceremony. Tessa continued to come to see me for some time after graduating.

Some thoughts

In Tessa's case, she grew up thinking that she was an orphan and very much appreciated what her grandparents had done for her as replacement parents. But it took a while for her to come to terms with their deceptive behaviour. Initially, she was also wrongfully angry with her father, whom she thought had deprived her of those many years she could have spent with him. Eventually, she realised that he was not to blame. Although he wanted to separate from his alcoholic wife he really wanted to maintain a relationship with his daughter. It was really Tessa's grandparents who prevented her from having that relationship. They kept the truth from her. They had obviously lied with good intentions, but all was far from the truth and eventually exposed.

Hearing her friend's excitement of going out with her parents stirred up some long-standing, inert feelings about the loss of her own parents. She had never mourned their loss because as a young child she was incapable of doing this. Her replacement parents, namely her grandparents, did not allow her to grieve. Her minor breakdown was partly mourning the loss of her parents. To some extent, this would have been a false premise as her father was alive. The shock of discovering the truth traumatised her and she had to go through the process of mourning the loss of her mother and the loss of not knowing her father during her childhood and teens. She also had to learn to forgive her grandparents before she felt emotionally stable to carry on with her own life.

3

SLEEPING WITH THE ENEMY

Bertha waited for Marek at the lakeside. It was a beautiful, bright sunny morning, which made the blue water look even bluer. Watching the gentle, symmetrical ripples, she was tempted to throw in a pebble to disrupt the harmony, as she and Marek had often done during their childhood. Nostalgically, she thought of those wonderful family picnics in the summer and skiing on the tarmac playing areas in the winter. She gave a sigh, knowing that those days would never return. Unkempt greenery and weeds intermingled with some of the perennials that kept coming up, surrounding the lake. The tarmac was broken all over with weeds, taking over wherever they could.

She had met Karl, her husband, here one evening when out with a group of friends and their parents. The cool evening after a stifling hot summer's day had tempted them out. Karl was visiting some relatives, who were also doing the same, relieved to be enjoying the gentle breeze. They were married by the end of that year. She was only twenty and he, twenty-two. She fondly touched the gold chain with a Star of David pendant he had given her, his first present, which he had lovingly fastened around her neck. She never took it off. Her parents became as fond of him as they were of Marek, Bertha's older brother.

Marek estranged himself from the family when he married Eva whom his parents were not keen on because she was a Christian.

Suddenly reminding herself how dangerous it was standing here on her own, Bertha looked around anxiously. German soldiers could appear at any time. She shivered even though it was a warm, sunny morning and, wrapping her shawl closely around her shoulders, she wondered where Marek was. He was always late. She had left the house soon after Karl had gone to work because Marek had insisted that she did not tell Karl about their meeting. She felt afraid. Marek had sounded so secretive. What was he up to now? Then, at last, there he was, striding along in his leisurely way. Giving her a big hug, he sat her down on the huge rock that was often used as a seat. He took out an envelope from inside his jacket and gave it to her.

"These are Eva's papers. Now, listen carefully." As he had handed them to her, he looked a bit nostalgic and briefly wiped away a tear. His late wife, Eva, a Hungarian national, had died after being seriously ill. It had all happened so quickly. She was six months' pregnant and he was devastated. His parents had never been keen on the marriage and unspoken guilty feelings were experienced on all sides. Bertha looked shocked and gazed at him blankly. He explained that as they were of no use now, she could use them to get out of the country. He said he had already discussed all this with their parents.

"All?" Bertha repeated, to which he informed her that he had tried to persuade their parents that he could get false identity papers and they could escape together to Switzerland before it was too late. Mother had similar fair colouring and features, inherited by both Bertha and Marek, and could easily get away. However, she had refused, saying that their father would never get away with his prominent Jewish features. She suggested that he help Bertha and Karl.

Looking at her tenderly and shaking his head, Marek said, "As you know, neither would Karl. You and I should go. You would have no problems with Eva's papers."

Without pausing, he went on to explain what they needed to do. She must not tell Karl and they could secretly escape that very night. There was no time to waste. He knew of someone who was going very close to the border and would give them a lift. Then, they could decide how to continue. According to the truck driver, several people whom he had given a lift to had escaped successfully. Bertha wondered how he would know that, but, too confused, she remained silent. If they were stopped, they had the documents. Bertha, shocked, shook her head and said she could not leave Karl. Marek tried to gently persuade her, but she refused. Losing patience, he angrily shouted. "The Nazis will get you." She freed herself from his grasp and ran towards home.

He called out, "You stupid fool. Go back to Karl and they will get you."

When Bertha entered the house, she flopped on the sofa and cried. After some time, she stood up and the envelope dropped from her lap onto the floor. Stunned, she picked it up and opened it to find a birth certificate, a marriage certificate and several other documents. Mindlessly, she shoved them back into the envelope, looked around and placed them at the bottom of a drawer. Several months went by and she almost forgot the envelope. But when her parents mentioned that Marek seemed to have disappeared, the scenario at the lakeside came back to mind. She remembered the envelope and wondered if he had managed to get to Switzerland. She did not tell them of her meeting with Marek. She knew that they really cared about him.

By now, the Germans were appearing everywhere, but snatches of news about the allies also brought some hope. People dreaded and listened for those heavy footsteps. Her parents had gone to hide with friends at a distant village. She never heard from them. Karl suggested that they try to do the same, but how? They had left it too late. Karl stayed home during the day and went out briefly during the night. They awaited those footsteps and the door being roughly pushed open. Thoughts about successfully getting away with Karl preoccupied her. Then without making the effort she found herself thinking about her chances of getting away. That thought at times was followed with, *I could not do that.*

One night, she was awake well into the early hours of the morning. The envelope kept invading her thoughts. She looked at the clock. It was three forty-five. She looked at Karl. He was fast asleep. She quietly slid out of bed, dressed, threw a few items of clothes into an old satchel and, opening the drawer quietly, found the envelope. She must be quick before the neighbours arose. As she looked up, she saw herself in the mirror and the gold chain with the star pendant dangled in front of her. She quickly took it off and left it on the dressing table. Without giving another glance at Karl, she quietly walked out. As she passed the spare room, she saw the small typewriter Karl had bought her when she said she wanted to learn to type. She picked it up and bundled it into a towel, slung it over her shoulder and walked out of the front door.

* * *

The live-in companion, a woman in her fifties, smiled at Bertha. She said she would return in an hour and left. Bertha was a tall, slim, white-haired woman; she was a little frail but retained some of her beautiful features. Her high cheekbone structure would be the envy of many a woman. At eighty-eight, there was still an air of elegance as she spoke softly but distinctly. She had blue eyes, had obviously been a blonde and was probably very beautiful in her younger days. She was a cultured woman and still went to concerts and the theatre. She lived in a luxurious apartment in a very desirable part of town. A daily help cleaned, shopped and cooked their meals, including her luncheon parties, which she seemed to have enjoyed until recently. Her two sons, a daughter and their respective families saw her regularly. They made sure she was comfortable.

What problems could a fortunate woman like her have? A few months ago, Bertha and her companion had been in a large department store. They had done some shopping and then as usual had lunch there. The companion noticed that Bertha looked a bit distracted and hardly ate her lunch. She thought no more about it,

----

but as they walked out, the alarm at the door went off. The security man stopped them and took them aside to check their bags. To the companion's horror, he took out several small items with the security tags still on including some pretty nightwear from Bertha's bag. They were taken to a side office. After much questioning – unsuccessfully, because Bertha could not stop crying and was shaking so much – the kindly young manager let them go. The manager whispered to the companion that Bertha was probably suffering from dementia and suggested she took her to her doctor. She suggested that in future she checked the old lady's bag before leaving the store. "If it ever happens again, the police will be brought in." The companion could not wait to get out with Bertha.

Driving home, she thought about how Bertha had been behaving a little strangely recently and recalled her preoccupation during lunch. She seemed to have days when she drifted into a world of her own. Puzzled and still shocked, she also recalled that Bertha had recently said some odd and disconnected things unexpectedly. She wondered if it was the beginning of dementia.

On returning home, Bertha said she felt very tired and went to lie down. The companion phoned her second son, who lived close by, giving him details of the morning's incident. The next day, she was taken to see her doctor and various tests followed.

* * *

For over three months, Bertha was brought to me regularly by her companion. Some days, she was full of the concerts or plays she had been to, her luncheon parties and her grandchildren. On other days, she seemed in deep thought but refused to share them, shaking her head or saying that it was nothing. Unexpectedly her son phoned, saying his mother was refusing to go out like she used to. She stopped giving luncheon parties. He was curious about her meetings with me and wanted to know if she was making any progress. "She looks forward to seeing you." Without trying to be dismissive or relate anything she had confided to me, I avoided answering his questions. Instead, I told him that it took time for clients to divulge what was worrying them in therapy. Often, people feel unclear as to what was making them feel anxious or distressed. It takes time before they themselves know or want to share their private thoughts with someone else. There was something on her mind that was disturbing.

A few weeks after my conversation with Bertha's son, she said, accusingly, "My son spoke to you. He worries too much. I can take care of myself without him. He does not have to interfere." She paused briefly and then went on to tell me about something she had read in the newspaper. It was horrid. Some women had been trapped in a house and abused. They were chained like dogs. She could not sleep all night, but stayed quietly in her room, not wanting to disturb the companion. Her mind was racing with images from the past.

I intuitively understood that there were several thoughts going through her mind. Her son had spoken to me. Could she trust me? Would I repeat all that she told me? The news in the paper obviously disturbed her and could she trust me enough to divulge the effect the news had on her to keep her awake all night. I repeated my thoughts to her. Tearfully, some of the incidents of her past life were related over the next weeks. They had remained her secret for many, many years.

"As I became more and more anxious about our safety I kept thinking about the envelope. Then one night when Karl was asleep I looked at the documents a few times. It was becoming dangerous as the Germans were rounding up the Jewish population and sending them to separate male and female camps. The sight of my husband's Jewish features felt threatening and this depressed me. I asked myself: 'Why did he so obviously look Jewish?'

"I started to hate him and could not bear to look at him any longer. One night, when he was fast asleep, I took off the gold chain with the Star of David pendant for the first time. I really did not think about what I was doing. I placed it in an envelope with a farewell note, stating that I would contact him through the central post office in Geneva when all this was over. He must make sure to go there. I carefully packed a few items and left in the dark to join a Hungarian women's camp. It was my only means of escape and survival. Fortunately, with my non-Jewish looks and false documents, I was accepted and allocated a bunk bed at the unit. The women worked at various factories and were given certain chores. I avoided making close friends and continually feared that my real identity might be discovered. What if someone I knew from my town came to the camp!"

Bertha paused, drank some water and remained silent for some time. She leaned back and shut her eyes. Then, gasping and rocking forwards and backwards, she whispered, "I can't go on! I can't go on! No! No! No!"

Eventually, between sobbing and long pauses, I gathered the following:

Some months after her stay in the camp, Bertha was transferred to work on a farm and was allocated the task of taking produce from the main storeroom to the officers' mess. On one of these trips, a young, handsome German officer was on duty. He helped her with the heavy bag. She did not understand his German and he spoke no Hungarian. Eventually, she gathered that he wanted the number of her unit. She somehow related the number of her unit and felt terrified that he was going to complain about her inadequacy to carry out her job.

Bertha continued, "The next morning, I awoke to find this beautiful head of blond, curly hair next to mine. He smiled, kissed me on the lips and left. From there on, he came regularly. One night, when he did not turn up, I kept looking out for him in the dark. At the time, I did not feel guilty, although I often thought about my husband. I felt if I refused the German, he could do anything to destroy me. During these meetings, neither of us said a word. He always brought me some sort of delicacy."

She paused, looked around the room then directly at me as if trying to understand what I was making of her confession. I repeated her last comment encouragingly. Then she continued, saying, "Now I have told you so much I may as well tell you the rest. One night he did not come. I waited and waited. I never saw him again. We heard rumours that the allies were approaching and that we would soon be freed. I was very confused and hardly knew what would become of me."

When the allies arrived, Bertha disclosed her real identity of being Jewish to get away from Hungary. She kept the name she had acquired and was relieved to be sent to Austria before coming to Britain. She made no attempt to find her husband. She vaguely recalled hearing that the Jewish men were taken to a camp and that most of them had died. She assumed he was dead because the survivors were shot by the Germans before they left. She also felt she had betrayed him by sleeping with the enemy. She felt very guilty and decided that she wanted to start a new life with no past ties. Years later, when she was well settled in England she surreptitiously tried to find out about her parents and her brother. She was unable to trace any of them. After several unsatisfactory jobs, she found a secretarial post with a Jewish family-run company. She was then in her early thirties and married the family's only son, who ran the business. She confessed that she never loved this husband and married him for security. She never told him or anyone about her real past, just the bit about the papers her brother had given her and that she had known a young man who did not survive the invasion.

"I often thought about the 'blond, curly head' and what had happened to him. Did he survive and now had a family of his own or was he dead, like my first husband? It was a secret and I, at first, lived in dread that someday someone might recognise me. But it never happened. The past faded into the background as I led a very busy life. My husband's parents were very influential people in the community. As he was an only child, I inherited the family business. My husband died ten years ago. I was left very well off financially. He was a good man and I sometimes felt guilty about the way I treated him. When we were being intimate, I never really felt satisfied and imagined I was with the German. I would happily have gone off with him given the opportunity. He was the love of my life."

During her therapy, Bertha went back to inviting friends to lunch but never on the scale she used to entertain. They were a few friends she had known for many years. All of them had come to the UK as refugees. Not long after ending the therapy, Bertha celebrated her ninetieth birthday with her family and friends in her flat. Soon after, however, she had a fall and sadly had to be moved to a nursing home. She remained mentally alert until her death.

Some thoughts

Bertha, like many of the people I saw, felt her secrets had to be told before she died, but did not know how to disclose what she believed to be outrageous and unforgiveable behaviour. As she grew older, vivid memories of her past activities came to haunt her daily life. She felt tormented and behaved in a most uncharacteristic manner to draw attention to herself. Obviously, she was not aware of this intellectually, but acted out her feelings of wanting to be punished. Reading about the abuser probably instigated her unspoken past activities. Her guilty feelings had much to do with wanting to be punished.

What has all this information to do with her shoplifting? Bertha managed to keep her secrets and lies to herself for almost her entire lifetime, but they were irrepressible. The persecutory guilt remained. The memory of her past could not be blotted out and as the reality of death and dying came to the fore, she felt desperate to be punished for what she considered was wrongdoing. She felt that the most appropriate punishment would be to be sent to prison, like the abuser she had read about. She had been a nasty, deceitful person. She felt she should be treated as cruelly as she believed her husband and parents had been. They had loved her very much and she had betrayed them. How could she tell anyone that she had loved the German soldier? Although he was good to her, he belonged to the group who condoned and tortured her loved ones.

Considering the details of events that led to her behaviour, one could argue that she acted so because of self-preservation – a strong, instinctive characteristic in us. Understanding the historical events of the time, one can see that if she had not done what she had, she would have suffered the same plight as her husband and parents. She never knew what happened to her brother. She assumed that he was caught somewhere while escaping or died somewhere unaccounted for. Who are we to be judgemental about her behaviour? Falling in love has no given moment and is beyond our control, although we can dissuade ourselves from giving in to the feeling. Perhaps the German soldier also loved her, but circumstances prevented them from openly acknowledging this. She was then a very attractive woman. He was kind and attentive towards her. When some of these thoughts were related to Bertha, she became less restless. She acknowledged a sense of relief, but the guilt remained. At times, she would say how cruel she had been to her first husband. He had been such a loving man. Even worse, she never told the truth about her past to her second husband or to his family. They had always been so kind and generous to her. They all assumed she had been a single woman before she met them.

Although Bertha did not feel entirely free of her burdensome secrets, she felt less agitated and depressed. She felt remorse and clearly differentiated between the truth and her lies. Recognising this enabled her to mourn the loss of her parents and especially her first husband.

On one occasion, in jest, but also perturbed, she asked, "What will happen if both my husbands come to meet me as I enter the other world?" There was no answer to such a question and I facetiously replied that she may have to find a therapist over there to sort out that problem. I added that perhaps there may be three men to meet her. She was quick to see what I meant and smiled.

4

——————

BALLGOWNS, GUILT AND REGRET

Tom looked out of the kitchen window. It was bleak and wet, a typical overcast October evening. He was not looking forward to spending the whole weekend with Maggie and her doleful, understanding expression. She would probably fuss over the evening meal while he listened to the monotonous details of her workplace. He felt desperate to get away. Recently, he had been preoccupied and a nagging feeling had continually impinged upon his usual tranquil demeanour. It had become worse after George had laughingly mentioned an experience he had had. George related that he and a friend had been on a pub crawl a few weeks ago. They had walked into one pub and had unexpectedly discovered it was an extraordinary place full of mirrors. Several pairs of eyes turned towards them, either directly or surreptitiously. At first, they were puzzled. After chatting to a few people while drinking their beer, they finally realised where they were. It was a bar that gay men frequented. George had laughed heartily.

Still standing by the window, Tom was in deep thought, debating silently as to whether he should go or not. He had married Maggie when he was twenty-two and an immature young adult. She was then thirty-three and very pretty; a war widow with two young boys of six and three. He was so pleased when he had found board and lodgings in a comfortable three-bedroom terrace soon after arriving on the outskirts of London. Everything was going his way; he had a good job with a kind manager, and a pretty, young, blonde landlady who had two well-behaved children.

He had been faithful to Maggie for thirty-four years, against all his silent longings for something very different. Snapping out of a reverie, he said to himself, "I cannot bear another evening here with Maggie looking mournfully at me. She means well, but I feel claustrophobic. It's now or never!" Determinedly, he walked to the coat stand in the hall. Not stopping to think anymore, he grabbed his outer coat and, as he was putting it on, called out to Maggie, "I'm going to the library. It's late night tonight. Don't wait supper for me. I'll probably stop for a beer and have something to eat," and almost ran out of the house.

Maggie opened the fridge to see what she could have for supper. She decided on a jacket potato with some bacon and cheese. As she was preparing her meal, she silently thought, *Poor Tom! He looks so lost these days. I think he has something on his mind which he doesn't want to talk to me about. Perhaps he wants to be with a younger woman. I will never forget what he did for me and the boys. Danny's death was such a shock.*

She placed her plate on a tray and went to eat her solitary meal in front of the television. After listening to the news while automatically eating, she pushed the tray aside with almost half the dinner still on it. The picture on the screen became blurred and the newscaster's voice sounded a long way off.

What a shock it had been when Danny had first gone missing and then, three months later, when the war office informed her that he was dead. Her youngest child was just a baby and her father, who had been terminally ill, died soon after. What was she going to do with two young children and no job? She had mindlessly taken care of the children and cried herself to sleep every night. Her mother had died when she was twenty, not long after she met Danny. But then Danny and her father had been there to console her, and she managed to cope. It was one of her friends who suggested that she take in one or two boarders or let out rooms. The thought of people sleeping, cooking and eating in the same room abhorred her. They would permanently smell of grease. It must cling to their clothes. She decided instead to take on one boarder and see how she coped, before getting a second one.

An advert at the local corner shop brought Tom to her front door. She liked the look of him. He was clean-shaven, well-dressed, well-educated and well-mannered. He had a good job in the civil service. By the following weekend, he had moved in. To add to his favour, the children adored him. He had a way with them.

Life moved on smoothly for nearly a year, but then Tom returned from work one day to find Maggie crying in the kitchen. It would have been Danny's birthday and, without having given it any thought, Maggie had found herself preparing his favourite meal – roast lamb. When she realised what she was doing, she burst into tears. Tom consoled her and they stayed up talking, long after the boys had gone to bed. She related her past to Tom and eventually he took her upstairs to bed. She asked him to stay and he remained the whole night with her, cradling her in his arms as she slept. That was the beginning of more to come. Not long after, an intimate relationship started between them. Tom felt enthralled because she was the first woman in his life.

"Poor Tom, I will never forget the happiness and joy he brought to my life. He has always been so good to me and the boys. Sometimes, I wonder if Danny would have made such a kind husband and father. He did like being out with the boys while we girls had to make do with each other's company."

Giving a huge sigh, she snapped out of her reverie and looked at the TV screen. She switched it off, picked up her tray and walked into the kitchen. Back in the everyday world, she cleared up and prepared to get ready to read in bed.

* * *

Tom, almost blanking out and trying not to think about anything, hopped onto a bus going in the direction of the city centre. He walked along, his feet moving him towards the bar that George had mentioned. He knew where it was because he had passed it several times on the bus since George had pointed it out. Without stopping to think, he tentatively pushed the door open and walked directly to the bar and ordered a pint. The barman gave him a beaming, welcoming smile, saying something about the wet weather. Tom didn't really register any of it. He vaguely nodded, paid for his beer and walked to the next room. He sat at the nearest vacant table. He dared not look up. Eventually, when he did, he noted several faces discreetly looking at him. As George had said, there were more mirrors here than he had ever seen in any room, let alone a pub. George had laughingly related, "There will be no pretty chicks there!"

Tom was thinking that he would down his beer as quickly as possible and run out, when the man at the next table came up and greeted him, saying, "Not seen you here before. I'm Collin. May I sit down and join you?" Tom nodded and Collin sat down. He reminded himself that he had had a purpose in coming here and now he was here, he must will himself to stay. An hour later, and after a second pint, he agreed to meet Collin and some of his friends the following week.

* * *

Tom studied the road map carefully. He discovered that the next turning was the road to the cottage. He had told Maggie he was going to play bridge with some friends at a country club and that he had met these friends at the library. Poor Maggie had seemed so pleased that he had made friends and was going to enjoy a weekend with them. The thought almost made him turn the car and go back home. He stopped, took a few deep breaths and once more started the engine, thinking determinedly, *It's now or never*. He drove into the driveway and parked next to two other cars.

Collin came out immediately and greeted him heartily, saying, "The others are here." He then took Tom to his room, after introducing him to Eddie and James. After tea, they walked to the village store to return with delicacies and enough food and wine for the weekend. Collin busied himself with preparing the evening meal while Tom went up to have a rest before showering. He was surprised to see a beautiful, blue ballgown carefully draped over a chair with matching accessories. Puzzled, he shook his head and lay on the bed, before drifting off to sleep. About an hour later, there was a gentle knock on the door and Collin asked if he could come in.

Looking at the gown, Collin said, "Perhaps you hadn't expected this, but it makes it more fun. Eddie will also be wearing something similar. You won't be alone. I will help you get ready after your shower."

This was the beginning of Tom's adventures. From then on, he led a dual life that lasted over several years. An intimate relationship with Maggie had ceased, although they slept in the same room on twin beds. Maggie, in turn, realised that Tom had been hankering for something else, perhaps a younger, more exciting woman. She told herself that she would be pleased for him because he had done so much for her and her boys. He was a good man and although she still loved him, he should have whatever he desired. She could never be angry with him.

* * *

For Tom, visiting the day unit made a break from being at home on his own and eating a lonely lunch. Still active, he would talk to others and help with the clearing up. He also enjoyed the company of the carers, who stopped to chat with him. Some of the people attending the unit were depressed and he tried to avoid them. He was occasionally visited by his stepchildren and adolescent grandchildren.

One of his stepsons lived abroad and came to see him whenever he was in the UK. Tom told me that there was a time when this stepson tried to persuade him to go and live abroad with him and his family in a private wing attached to his big house. But Tom could not think of going to a strange country at his age, where everything would be unfamiliar.

He heard about psychotherapy unexpectedly and, to quote him, "I decided to give it a go! Then, one day, while talking to a young voluntary helper, I discovered that she was training to become a psychologist. I was very interested and after several brief conversations, I disclosed that I had some things on my mind that would not go away. Things I could not speak about to her or anyone else." The helper mentioned it to the consultant psychiatrist. Being a friend of mine, he arranged a short meeting for Tom to see me. Tom quickly confided that he had some very disturbing thoughts from his past that he remembers vividly and which haunt him. He said that they kept him awake during the night. I offered him an appointment for an initial assessment. The psychiatrist agreed that his insomnia was due to some unresolved emotional problems and that psychotherapy could help. Appropriate arrangements were made for him to see me, once a week.

Tom came to see me when he was eighty-one. I saw Tom for just over two years.

Tom's story

Tom, who was of small stature, was intelligent and smartly dressed. At our initial meeting, he said he was pleased to come, but was not sure whether anything could be done because, "It's all too late! Too late! Too late! You can't put the clock back. What has been done cannot be changed. I have to live with it for the rest of my life."

He was the only son. His parents had been in their forties when they married. Tom had been a sickly youth and survived a bout of pneumonia in his teens. At the age of twenty, he had lost both his parents, who died within months of each other. At twenty-two, Tom moved to London to take up a position in the civil service. It was then that he moved into Maggie's house as a boarder.

Not surprisingly, he was reluctant to say any more during our early meetings. His time was spent in relating his everyday activities, especially his time at the day centre, where he was given the opportunity to use a computer, which he loved. His stepson had promised to get him one as a birthday present. Time in our sessions passed with Tom relating trivialities, which were obviously very important to him. As his trust in me grew, he told me of his secret life of cross-dressing and his weekends with Collin, Eddie and James.

In relating his relationship with Maggie, he volunteered, "One thing led to another and we were married. I soon realised that it was a big mistake! I had been seduced. But she was a good woman and never complained. In fact, I was very fond of her and she was the kindest person I ever knew. I am also very fond of her children and they accepted me as a father – they are still good to me. I see them and their children regularly. One of them lives fairly close to me."

About six months into his sessions, he announced enthusiastically, "I can't believe this! I did not think it would be allowed! I found a website for gay men. It is very subtle but most interesting."

Following this disclosure, when he found I was not shocked by what he told me, encouraged him to speak about his previous double lifestyle. At first reluctantly, but when he found I was not being critical he continued without hesitation.

"The irony of it was that when Maggie became seriously ill, I could not leave her. I became preoccupied with suicidal thoughts, like dying with her. I had let her down. I now feel she must have guessed something about my secret and suffered in silence. There was never a complaint or a nasty word from her! She was a good woman. One day, I very much wanted to confess my secret to her, but she convulsed in pain and I could not tell her. Instead, I gave her the medication and she slept for a long time. Perhaps she instinctively guessed the truth. I sometimes feel I should have divorced her. That would have been kinder, as she could have met someone who loved her and treated her properly."

Several meetings later, he divulged that he regrets not having told Maggie the truth. After her death, he had felt guilty. He believed she had discovered his secret, which had made her ill. He was the cause of her death. The suicidal thoughts once more occurred. He could not bear to live in the house. Although the children inherited the house after Maggie's death, they wanted him to stay on, but he decided to move into a one-bedroom council flat. Oppressive thoughts haunted him for several months after Maggie's death. She was his soulmate. Although he was comfortable in the rented accommodation, he continually felt tormented. To quote him,

"There could not have been a lonelier person in the world. How I survived those years after the death of Maggie and Collin remains a mystery to me. Although the weekend parties had stopped a long time ago, Collin and I remained good friends. I lived a solitary lifestyle. I shopped, cooked and cleaned, until the grandchildren brought me some happiness. They are still very good to me and I really love them. Slowly, I started to socialise again but not in any big way."

Tom's secrets and lies remained somewhat dormant as time passed, until one day they came flooding back. He was walking back from the cinema when he saw some ballgowns for hire in a window. There was something odd about the whole display. The dresses were displayed as theatrical costumes for amateur actors. Out of curiosity and instinct, Tom felt as though he was being led into the store. It was a junkshop full of women's clothes and accessories. When the owner come out from a backroom and smilingly asked if he could help, Tom felt a shiver run down his spine. He recognised what kind of a shop it was, shook his head and could not get out quickly enough. It was obviously for transvestites. Memories came flooding back and had been haunting him ever since. They keep him awake for hours. Since Collin, he had never had another relationship with anyone. A few times, he had been tempted to go back to the bar where they had met, but he could not carry this out. The people he had met through Collin seemed to disappear, and he never saw or heard anything about them again. Somehow, that chapter remained forever closed. He was in his late sixties at this stage.

During another of our sessions, Tom confided that something infrequently stirred inside him. They were feelings he never verbalised, even to himself. They terrified him whenever they occurred, but for the first time he felt that he could talk about them. With lots of pauses, he divulged that an inner voice said that if he carried out his illicit behaviour again, he would be the cause of death to that person. He believed his behaviour was the cause of Maggie's death. This thought petrified him. He had no desire to be with anyone again. He decided never to go into that website and asked his granddaughter to take away the computer. He was happy to use the one at the day centre instead. He would not be able to search on that website.

Some thoughts

I always feel very sad when I think about Tom. He was unfortunate to be born during an era when transvestites and homosexuality was considered a sin, unlawful and the consequence could be punishment. As a young, kind, vulnerable man, his first experience of a sexual relationship was with an older, motherly woman. When he discovered his real sexual need, it was denied. For a long time, he remained faithful to Maggie. Circumstances and societal values had to be maintained. He married Maggie and chose a path that he would probably never have chosen if he had been alive during our current time. His hero was Oscar Wilde, who often came up during his sessions, although Tom never looked at young boys. Fortunately, he did not suffer the same plight as his hero, but his whole life was a sham that brought about unhappiness intermingled with some happier times. At the time of our meeting, he attended a local day unit for the elderly, which he enjoyed. He remained with Maggie until her death in the same small terraced house. She became accustomed to his bridge weekends and never questioned him about them. Sometimes, he wished to confess the truth and a few times came close to doing so. However, he felt he could not hurt Maggie's feelings, but often wondered if she suspected he was lying.

As a young man, Tom's childhood and adolescence was not altogether a happy one. His illness left him dependent on his parents. Then, losing them at such a young age had probably affected him more than he had realised. He was a needy young man when he met Maggie, who comes over as an understanding, motherly figure, who had had to face her own sadness following the loss of her husband. Further still, she had to bring up two young children on her own and their demands had not given her the space needed to mourn her husband's death. She also sounded like a practical person, capable of getting on with the necessary demands made on her. Tom, a vulnerable, needy young man, complimented her characteristics. They fitted like two opposites; one was able to give and the other take without being detrimental to each other. While Tom became the replacement husband, Maggie fulfilled the role of the mother figure that he needed. Like a mother, she instinctively knew what he needed. Maggie was aware that Tom was hankering after something. She presumed it to be the companionship of someone younger and more exciting than her. But what she never, perhaps, guessed was that he was gay and craved a relationship with a male.

The pressure of societal values and Tom's guilty feelings about being unfaithful to Maggie preoccupied his later years. The recollection of what he considered as abhorrent behaviour worried him. He was also preoccupied with the thought that if he started a relationship with another man, it would be the death of that man. Perhaps this feeling was associated with guilt and was a way of preventing himself from going back to his secret lifestyle.

5

GROWING OLD
AND LATER LIFE

Guilt, reparation, grieving, remorse, mourning and melancholia

Anthony Powell, a writer and keen admirer of Marcel Proust, visited and stayed at some of the places mentioned in Proust's novel. He said, "Growing old is like being increasingly paralysed for a crime you haven't committed." Studies on ageism indicate that people are living longer, well into old age. Their expectations and demands are also growing. Retirement, for many, is a period to fulfil needs and wishes that they were unable to achieve while employed or involved with family commitments. Facilities for further education, travelling and many other activities are readily available for this age group. Many appreciate and have grown accustomed to enjoying this phase. However, ageing is unavoidably a chronological process and is quite often a physically degenerative time for many. Unavoidable illnesses of either a serious nature or of a milder kind are experienced. Modern technological treatments and medical intervention are more readily available, help many people to overcome various disorders and illnesses, and has prolonged the lifespan. Still, growing old is also a stage when one is confronted with the inevitable prospect of death and dying. At this late stage of the lifespan, the reality of death becomes more significantly evocative, and is perhaps anticipated by many with some perplexity and trepidation. Thoughts of death, previously from an intellectual perspective, exacerbate to become a personal emotional activity. Loss of partners, family members and friends intensify the subject. Furthermore, the anxieties about not knowing how soon, when or where this will happen can also be alarming and depressing. When we are born, regardless of our background, life's misfortunes or successes, the only certainty is that we will inevitably die one day.

Ageism and its related complexities can become overwhelmingly problematic for providers. Catering for the welfare and wellbeing of the elderly engenders defeatist thoughts in many organisations. Concentration often swivels around cognitive, behavioural and external provision. Although it is undoubtedly necessary, many providers overlook or fail noting of 'inner states' or emotional needs. Every old person was once an infant, who was cradled and nurtured, then a child, an adolescent, before reaching adulthood and eventually becoming old. Throughout these stages of lifetime, they experience all kinds of feelings. Circumstances, especially during a crisis, may have made many behave in a manner that is alien to their usual nature. Spontaneity is a part of human behaviour. It can come to the fore, activated by pleasurable feelings or perhaps be a reaction to a difficult situation. With hindsight, some of these activities may later be regretted or even disowned. The necessity for self-preservation motivates several kinds of actions. These may differ from one's normal behavioural patterns. The truth of the situation becomes peripheral and unimportant at the time, but sooner or later, when the reality of the experience is acknowledged, it brings on the guilt and makes the person feel unworthy or even nasty, as the stories in Section One indicated.

During the later stage of life, many who seemed like contented people, living a good, healthy lifestyle, are in emotional turmoil. Their families may not have noticed or are ignorant of their states of mind. Some older people feel burdened with some of the responsibilities they need to attend to. Perhaps a lost partner used to see to these activities, which they now need to confront on their own. Although many older adults love and care for their grandchildren, it may be too difficult for them to cope with the demands of young children. Some may feel that they have been foisted upon and are too afraid to tell the truth. They secretly fear the consequences of the relationship with their children.

For example, a client who came to see me briefly was referred after she had several falls. No physical reason could be found for this. She was a healthy woman in her late sixties, had a busy social life and generally enjoyed getting around. She could not understand why this was happening. She wore sensible shoes and tried to be careful and watched where she was stepping. It transpired that she usually picked up her younger grandchild from the local school, which was within walking distance. She loved doing this and they often went to the park or to a local café. Unexpectedly, the daughter-in-law asked her if she could also fetch the older child. This meant collecting the younger child and then drive on to pick up the older girl, take her first to her various after school activities before bringing both home. She was also told that she could treat the younger one at a nearby café, while waiting for the older one. She agreed, but soon found the initial pleasurable activity became a daunting task. She hated driving to the other side of the town. The roads were busy at that time with parents driving their children back from school. She was unable to refuse or discuss her feelings with her daughter-in-law. She silently dreaded the afternoons and the previous pleasurable activity became a nightmare.

She herself was not aware of the connection. The falling was linked to her fear of driving in heavy traffic. She was unable to refuse doing what she hated so much. This was not the only reason. There were connected feelings regarding her relationship with her daughter-in-law. Although she was kind and generous, she had a way of ordering

----

people around in a subtle but forceful way. My client had noticed this characteristic in her and found it difficult to refuse her request. Some fears and anxieties that seem like 'just a nuisance' when one is younger become more problematic as one grows older. At times, these little anxieties exacerbate to become burdensome. One may be aware of these changes but emotionally refuse to accept the ageing process and its limitations.

Preoccupation with long-term memory may increasingly involve the recollection of pleasant but also unsavoury past activities. The past can intrude on mental wellbeing during later life. Physical impairment is easier to accept as part of the ageing process. Past misconduct, which is trapped in an emotional time machine, comes as a shock when recalled. Suddenly, those blurred, indistinguishable memories of the past become dramatically intrusive. They evoke distressing feelings. As the earlier related stories indicate that although well stored for many years and left in abeyance, the pressure to confess intensifies. However, there was also the desire not to hurt loved ones.

For those who lived decent lives, their previous negative behaviour may feel too painful, disgusting and abhorrent to be tolerated. They could not be kept any longer as secrets. Recalling from the past may not be precise, but nevertheless it can be disturbing. Institutionalised old people tend to say things that are totally unconnected with the present. This may be blurted out uncontrollably and mistaken as mental disturbances through ageing, or wild imagination and phantasy. Family members, others and carers may fail to recognise that the unpredictable behaviour or anecdotes stem from internal sources of real past activities. These disturbances may seem eccentric or idiosyncratic.

Care staff are not often trained to see beyond the biological, physical and external needs of the elderly. Unless one is intuitive or insightful, one often mistakes negative emotional activities as bizarre and tends to ignore them. Obviously, psychoanalytic knowledge and training is required to ascertain emotional dysfunctional difficulties. Some of this is now being included in the training of care staff. Nevertheless, sympathetic understanding is not beyond the capacity of most people. Listening does not require training. Forms of behaviour like feeling low, unsociable or being depressed, which are outwardly obvious, should be easily recognisable. Discovering or interpreting inner turmoil, understandably would not be easy to piece together for the untrained. Unfortunately, many care homes and institutions for the old are understaffed. Abuse of the elderly is known to occur in some places. Care staff members undergo an immense amount of pressure. They work long hours, sometimes caring for very difficult old people. Therefore, supervision and support to create some awareness of emotional behaviour should be an essential for care staff.

When one is enjoying a delightful and what seems like a good lifestyle, especially during adulthood, long-suppressed and unwanted feelings may remain dormant. Previous wrongdoing, if recalled, may be logically argued and believed that circumstances necessitated such behaviour. However, disturbing secrets cannot be discarded as irrelevant. There is the truth and *the truth* and every experience remains in our unconscious in its *true* form. Did one's desires, ambitions and need for survival stay with *the truth* or are there connected guilt feelings floating around? During old age, it seems as if those experiences suddenly return to disturb some, emotionally. During my work with older adults, I discovered that frequently or occasionally nagging feelings tormented their peace of mind. Many avoided or 'pushed back' these provocative thoughts. They were left in abeyance to be confronted and dealt with at some later stage. Often, the fact that they had lied instigated some guilty feelings.

For some old people, as their remaining lifespan gets shorter, they find those undesirable and long-forgotten experiences oppressive. As well as coping with the physical ageing process, it is also a time for emotional and mental adjustments. Old people may feel under an immense amount of internal pressure to confess these unspoken, well-kept secrets before it is too late. Death is an unknown quantity that entails all kinds of illusions, mysteries and fears. For some, disturbing feelings of what the afterlife may involve evokes fears and anxieties. To confess,previously inadmissible secrets becomes urgent.

Fortunately, many tolerate and accept their past as the dynamics of human everyday activities. Horrendous behaviour towards others needs to be reassessed, regretted and grieved. Feelings of remorse play a vital role in achieving peace of mind or tranquillity. This does not mean that all old people divulge or are bothered by negative experiences. Many remain continually in denial and take their secrets to their grave. The people discussed earlier felt overwhelmed and disturbed by what they felt was their abhorrent past. They became mildly depressed or physically unwell. The urgency to talk about their secrets and lies before they died became an obsession. The fear of condemnation, chastisement or that they may become targets of ridicule and contempt also prevented them from seeking help earlier.

A state of despair from not being able to tell anyone their secrets unbalanced their previously relaxed lifestyle. Some behaved irrationally and acted out their feelings to seek attention. From my clinical experience, I think that although they had not realised this, the failure to mourn their past unsavoury activities played a role in them seeking help. The secrets, lurking around in their minds, had to be confronted. They needed to tell someone before they died.

Critics of the 'false memory syndrome' may renounce some of the stories given in Section One and explain them as coming from the imagination rather than reality. Within the traditional analytical/psychotherapeutic practice, this is accepted and understood. Well-repressed, indigestible, disturbing, early experiences often do come to the fore in the conducive environment of the consulting room. However, it could be argued that these vivid recalled memories may be distorted, far from the truth or phantasies. But why should old people undergoing such distress be prevented from talking about what they believe as their experiences, if it brought about relief at this late stage? False, confused and/or distorted states of mind they may be, but the point is that they have disrupted their emotional well-being. 'False memory syndrome' does exist, as discussed in the next section. The aim should be to give them the opportunity to use 'the talking cure' without colluding, which may help them lead a more enhanced, happier lifestyle.

Guilty feelings can be a powerful internal feature for many people who have committed some activity that is dishonest or against their character. Although their intentions were well meant, any falsehood involved may remain on their conscience and later evoke uncomfortable feelings. Making *reparation* through apologising or exposing their behaviour to the others concerned is usually the straightforward way. But reassessing one's actions or behaviour may not always be straightforward or simple. Consequences may be painful to the recipient, causing undue unhappiness. They may also involve other innocent people. Under these circumstances, perhaps the solution may be to sincerely acknowledge one's actions, *grieve* and feel some *remorse* for what had been done during an impulsive moment. By doing this, integration can take place.

Mourning and melancholia are not only connected with death. These internal processes are also connected with times when one is undergoing personal, physical and emotional losses. Feelings of melancholia or states of feeling sad, depressed, distressed and anxious are linked with many kinds of losses. These may be experienced by anyone at any stage of one's lifetime. It involves a state of grieving that varies with the individual's mental capacity. Recognising this state and beginning to work through it is the process of mourning. The most extreme form of it is the loss of a loved one through death. The mourning or grieving period differs from person to person. Integration slowly takes place before emotional tranquillity is regained. If the individual is unable to work through the melancholic state and remains in stasis, depression sets in.

Unfortunately, this state of mind, which is common among old people, is not always easily recognised or treated because mourning is generally associated with the death of someone. In the psychoanalytic/psychotherapeutic profession, mourning is linked with emotional losses as Freud first introduced. Care staff with well-meant intentions, encourage depressed or anxious old people to be involved with activities or social events to 'jolly them along'. These are peripheral activities that may temporarily relieve the situation, but do not help inner change or satisfaction. Growing old or being old is not necessarily 'too late to become the person you might have been' as George Eliot wrote. The gist of this is encouraging but in truth there are some limitations as to what you really can achieve due to the physical ageing process. I also think that one should learn to forego, forgive and move forward. There are many people with various kinds of disabilities who have reached old age and live fulfilled lives. The pioneer of psychoanalysis, Sigmund Freud, who suffered physical ill health, worked and lived until his death at the age of eighty-three. His philosophy was to think positively. He stated, 'One must try to learn something from every experience.' This, I feel, should be the incentive as one reaches the later stages of life.

SECTION TWO

OUR INNER LIFE

The practice of psychotherapy is an involved process of trying to understand the mind, psyche or 'inner self' and how this impacts an individual. Modernism and the media in the twenty-first century has invasively and intrusively infiltrated many areas of knowledge. However, some subjects, to this day, remain exclusively the province of professionals. I think psychotherapy is one of them because of the intricate learning process involved. Although many training schools now offer courses on the subject to create some awareness to those working in other humane fields, such as nursing, social work and teaching, it is still an enigma to many. Perhaps this is because the clinician is trained to acquire the subtle ability to listen, observe and be insightful to the feelings connected to the experiences of the patient. Simultaneously, the psychotherapist is constantly aware of her learned knowledge of psychoanalytic theory, linking this to what the patient is saying and conveying her understanding of the problem in simple language to the patient when necessary. The interpretation may be shared immediately or at a later, more appropriate time. The patient is free to accept, deny or dispute the interpretation. Ideally, the patient should be encouraged if possible, to recognise his problem.

One may argue that other professionals like doctors, nurses, physiotherapists also interpret what they think is the problem of the patient. The difference is that they are dealing with pain linked to something more obviously concrete. They accept the diagnosis immediately, except in rare cases and trust the clinician to help alleviate the pain. Feelings cannot be concretely seen and as previously discussed, are transient and therefore more difficult to pinpoint to a given moment.

Since the establishment of psychoanalysis, many forms of psychological therapies are now in practise and therapeutic treatment has become more accessible, but most people still do not understand how it works. Psychoanalytic literature is far more difficult to understand because much of it is about the functioning of the mind and an inanimate, non-visible entity. Most of the literature is written in theoretical jargon about an invisible 'inner world'. Unlike other humane treatments it is to do with thinking about one's feelings, an experiential activity which is often incomprehensible to the lay reader. It requires an intellectual frame of mind that is open to the understanding and interpretations of experiential activities, triggered off by the senses of the psyche or 'inner self'. Feeling, an experience that we all undergo during our daily lives, is taken for granted. Many hardly question what feelings are about? Why do we recall and remember unwanted experiences from the past, that are of no use to us during the present? Why do we need to feel? The following pages are an attempt to create some awareness about these questions in as simplified a form as possible. This is in no way trying to undermine a very complicated profession, which requires many years of arduous training. It is to extend some basic thoughts and themes about our feelings to a wider understanding of a subject, which has been an enigma to many.

Most literature on the subject is written by clinicians to share their thoughts with colleagues or for those training in the field. This is probably due to the importance of confidentiality (mentioned in Section One) required as part of a verbal contract understood between the clinician and the patient. Trust plays a significant role in enabling the patient to speak about some very private feelings which he/she does not want to be made public. The process of psychoanalysis, psychotherapy, analysis – varied expressions used by the different institutions – is basically working at looking at the 'inner self', psyche or personality of the patient/client. The psychotherapist is also trained to unobtrusively listen in a non-judgemental, uncritical manner, encouraging the patient to speak about what is troubling him. The ultimate aim is to encourage the client to find his true identity.

I have often found during social gatherings that the moment I mention I am a psychotherapist, it can be a conversation stopper. Some people jokingly enquire if I am silently analysing everyone around. Some walk away or avoid getting into a conversation with me. Others make cynical remarks and laugh at their own jokes. Any word beginning with the prefix 'psycho', such as psychoanalysis, psychotherapy, psychology or psychodynamics seem to make people immediately feel uncomfortable. Like other professionals, analysts separate their working life from their private and social lives.

Our multifaceted psychic or internal world is not altogether as mysterious as one may imagine and can be understood if desired. Although our daily lives are impacted with feelings, many are not curious enough to want to learn more. Some who look confident become afraid when disturbing thoughts and feelings invade their peace of mind. Writing on the subject is also an attempt to remove the stigma still attached, if one needs such support to help with emotional difficulties. Scepticism also still prevails, especially with those who try to understand therapeutic intervention from a purely intellectual stance. Psychotherapy helps to gain insight into one's feelings when one's lifestyle is disrupted with unwelcome, inexplicable, troublesome thoughts. People are often bewildered when they fail to make sense of these thoughts, which they cannot easily forget and fail to understand why they feel haunted by them.

Government authorities recognise these dysfunctional states of mind under the wider umbrella of mental illness. Providers, however, are still reluctant to acknowledge psychotherapy on a bigger scale to help such people, although it is a more humane form of treatment without the side effects of antidepressants. The latter often helps to calm and alleviate the symptoms temporarily. Some people continue to take medication as the root of the problem is not found or seriously considered. Whereas psychotherapy attempts to locate the source of the problem and thus help to heal the person. The study of mental processes as conveyed in psychoanalytic theory is complicated and often intangible, compared to that of the physical anatomy. When unbearable or incomprehensible experiences from the past continually invade one's tranquillity, the body often takes on the pain, to relieve the strain on the mind. In analytical literature this is referred to as somatisation. As indicated in Section One some of the case studies somatised their unbearable experiences. Mild depression, emotional stress and anxiety are states of mind due to some negative feelings linked with either earlier or current invasive experiences, unfathomable to the person. However, to learn about them as Proust suggested, 'one should not seek new lands but new eyes'.

The practice of psychotherapy, as explained in Chapter 11, is long, intensive and an arduous training over several years. The training involves learning to scrutinise and to understand any underlying in-depth feelings that may exist and be the root of the patient's problem. Psychotherapeutic involvement is a humane, person-centred approach of listening and observing without being intrusive. The psychotherapist, I repeat, acts as a catalyst to support the patient to become aware of whatever is troubling him and make adjustment for the improvement of the 'inner self'. As conveyed in Section One, working through negative feelings and activities instead of denying or disregarding them requires some intricate and involved psychic changes, not always possible to achieve on one's own.

Generally, people seek support for physical health readily when needed. They willingly improve their cognitive skills. But many refrain from seeking help for emotional/mental well-being. Many do not see that emotional/mental well-being and physical good health are often interdependent. Coping with adverse feelings associated with the *truth* if the experience has been too painful and unbearable, understandably makes it difficult for many to seek help. Some people believe they should be able to deal with their problem or if avoided by trying to push it away, it will sooner or later disappear. Others feel reluctant to see an analyst because of the connected feelings of shame. As mentioned earlier the internal problem may manifest itself as a bodily ailment through somatisation, resulting in anything from a headache to more serious condition. Consequently, they seek medical help. How do we know this? Anna's story (The Walnut Trees – in Section One) is one example. Exploring through the person-centred activity helps the patient to concentrate and consider his feelings and thoughts. The psychotherapist could perhaps be thought of as a handyman who uses the appropriate tools to carry out a task. Without the tools, the task at hand becomes futile and the problem remains. Therefore, I hope these pages will encourage more people not to despair but seek psychotherapeutic support. I stress and clarify that by no means am I stating that all physical illnesses are due to somatisation.

As in Section One, reconstructed vignettes are given to clarify some of the connections made with theoretical concepts, to create a broader understanding of a complicated and intricate subject.

Chapter 6, the first in this section, has been deliberately chosen to give an account of some therapeutic work involving an adolescent. His experiences of 'acting out' his irrepressible feelings, will perhaps help readers to understand how unbearable emotional pain is sometimes dealt with. Although this can be an experience at any age the example is that of an adolescent who 'acted out' emotional pain.

This is followed with a chapter related to the subject of feelings as experienced by the late nineteenth-century novelist, Marcel Proust, in his long novel: *Remembrance of Things Past*. He preoccupied himself with observing, listening and interpreting the behaviour of the people he associated with. He believed they were 'acting out' and that they were hiding their 'true thoughts and feelings'. The novel is full of his interpretations of the characters he associated with during social occasions. This sounds pompous and arrogant but given careful consideration as to what and why he came to such conclusions is interesting.

During the same century, Sigmund Freud (1) the pioneer of psychoanalysis, studied the feelings of hysterical women in a methodical manner. Initially he had been influenced by the finding of a colleague, Josef Breuer, who used hypnosis as a method of treatment for his hysterical female patients to alleviate their mental stress. Breuer discovered that encouraging them to talk about some of their experiences whilst he listened, relieved much of their hysteria. Freud and Breuer (2) together published *Studies on Hysteria (1895)*. Breuer had given up this method of working some time ago. Freud actively continued working in this manner and furthered the technique. He listened and carefully observed his patient for any bodily nuances, reactions and feelings displayed. Freud dogmatically and systematically later scrutinised the notes he had made immediately after each meeting with a patient. He seriously thought and contemplated on what the patient had said as well as the feelings conveyed during the session. Therefore, this chapter concentrates on some general discussion of the various kinds of feelings human beings display. Feelings are part of our daily lives and a very important feature of psychotherapeutic intervention. The chapter aims to clarify some intricate psychoanalytic theory in simple language.

A further chapter discusses the human emotional/psychological development from birth to adulthood. It also discusses that language is part of us from a very early age when the cognitive skills develop and helps us with the rudiments of communication. Firstly, an infant imitates sounds and thereafter continually acquires cognitive comprehension. Unquestionably, we express our bodily and mental needs through the medium of language, originating from our feelings and universally accepted as the norm for communication. The sensual feelings we experience send signals that provoke thought or the thinking process, which ultimately leads to verbalisation. Throughout civilisation, language, no matter how rudimentary, has been the principal means of communication to express one's feelings and thoughts. Jacques Lacan, a keen exponent of mental functioning, said, 'Language gives to our experience a new solidity and strengthens the meaning.' The chapter further discusses some of the emotional development during adolescence and adulthood.

Memory plays a significant role during our lifetime. In this chapter some basic points of a very complicated faculty are discussed. The activity of recalling and remembering from memory is demonstrated with examples to indicate the impact it can have on an individual.

Following this, the next chapter is called 'The Talking Cure'. It introduces some of the requirements needed to qualify as a psychotherapist. This involves both practical and experiential training and learning about some very intricate and involved activities of the psyche or 'inner self'.

Section Two finally concludes with some further thoughts that may be of interest to the reader.

The aim and reason for trying to explain the practice of psychotherapy in a simplified form and avoiding jargon is to encourage people who need support for emotional well-being to seek help. It is not to undermine the profession nor to create sensationalism. I repeat that it is to make an involved and difficult subject accessible to those who wish to understand the working of psychotherapy. It is also to make people aware that integration and reconciliation can only take place by forgoing and forgiving before one moves forward. Failure to do so creates emotional difficulties and prevents one from leading an enhanced, happier lifestyle.

6

ACTING OUT
IRREPRESSIBLE FEELINGS

Ben, a thirteen-year-old, was lonely and unhappy because he was continually teased, called a 'smelly idiot' and bullied at school. He became a loner and, although intelligent, was not performing to the best of his ability. Ben's father was an alcoholic and Ben witnessed many loud arguments between his parents. During one of those awful rows his father walked out when the mother threatened to call the police. For several years she had been the sole provider as the father did a few odd jobs and spent most of his earnings on alcohol. Ben was nine at the time. His father turned up infrequently to see him. As he was not allowed to come into the house they spent time together in the nearby park. He usually gave Ben some money before he left. On rare occasions they went to a cafe, but since Ben started at secondary school he refused to go out with him.

At our initial meeting, I noticed that Ben's mother was a sad, lonely woman and looked emotionally battered. She devoted her life to tending to her son's welfare. Much to Ben's annoyance, she disclosed that from about the time his father left, he sometimes wet the bed. Since moving to secondary school, this happens frequently. Ben refuses to see the doctor. To avoid embarrassing him, his mother had arranged that whenever this happened, he should leave the soiled linen in the washing machine to be laundered. She hoped he would grow out of it. Knowing how badly he had taken his father leaving, she had been tolerant and understanding.

Contradictory to his mother's belief, Ben had been aware of his father's alcoholism from a fairly young age. He clearly recalled the inebriated state he used to find his father in when he went into the bedroom to see him before school. He remembered seeing empty bottles on the floor and recalled that the room was very smelly. His mother slept in the living room and was usually up very early to get his breakfast ready. She used to get annoyed with Ben for going into the bedroom, saying that he should not disturb his father. Ben was unable to process these negative aspects of his father at such a vulnerable age. Instead, he made up stories to tell his peers of the great times he spent with his dad.

After about six months of regular weekly meetings with Ben who was often defensive and undermining of whatever I said, he started to come to his sessions with a small bottle of Coke. He usually placed it on the table next to him and intermittently took a sip as he observed me. After several repetitions of this simple act, I realised that he was trying to tell me something, which he found difficult to verbalise. He was silently conveying a message. Eventually, it occurred to me that the bottle of coke represented alcohol. He was imitating his father's habit that he found too painful to talk about. When I tentatively connected his actions with that of his father's alcoholism, he immediately and vehemently denied it as rubbish. Typical of adolescent behaviour he verbally abused me as the adult who thought I knew it all.

After a few weeks, he volunteered, "I like Coke. I buy a litre bottle every day after school and drink it through the night." He went on to inform me that he liked Coke very much and divulged that he hid it from his mother because she would disapprove and confiscate the bottle. She would be furious, as he was only allowed a small glass of water after his supper. He often felt very thirsty during the night.

It became obvious to me that the Coke resembled some of the alcoholic drinks his father consumed. Ben was re-enacting and imitating him. When I suggested that he was behaving like his father, by secretly buying and drinking Coke, bed-wetting and becoming smelly, he gave a short, hysterical laugh. As usual he went on to undermine any connections I made. After a pause I went on to say that his secret drinking during the night was perhaps his way of wanting to experience what it was like to be his father, get drunk, wet the bed and be smelly. He gave me a furtive glance and wriggled in his chair. After remaining quiet for a brief period, he suddenly burst out repeatedly, "Yeah! Yeah! I am like my father! I am smelly? I have no friends. Who cares?" By the end of his time with me he had calmed down but walked out without saying "Bye" as usual or looking at me.

This was a crucial stage of his therapy as it led him to share some of his anxieties and feelings about several issues. From there on, as his trust in me grew, he recognised and disclosed other connected feelings. He missed not having a 'proper father' and dreaded that his peers might find out about his father's alcoholism. He wished his father could be like other fathers.

Several sessions later, he came in looking exceedingly angry and threw his bag on the floor. It transpired that his mother had refused to allow him to stay up late to watch a football match. During past sessions, I had perceived some ambivalent feelings towards his mother, but this incident brought it to the fore. Their relationship was a difficult one under the circumstances, with a mother having to cope with a problematic adolescent. He loved his mother but was also angry with her for the way she had treated his dad. I tentatively suggested some of this to him. He remained silent as if agreeing with my comments. Encouraged, I went on to add that, perhaps there were also several other reasons. She was still treating him like a young child in refusing to allow him to watch TV late into the night, limiting how much he could drink before bedtime. Perhaps there were other complaints regarding her. He did not immediately respond, shrugged his shoulders and looked away.

After a short period of silence, I suggested that maybe at times I behaved like his mother. I made the rules as to when he could come to see me and when he had to leave. Looking at me piercingly, he responded, "Rubbish! Rubbish! Sometimes, you speak rubbish. You need to see a shrink! You think you know everything. Bloody hell! You know what's in my mind? Do you?"

This was followed with lots of jeering and laughter. I realised that I had touched on some truth. After his outburst, he abruptly became calmer and seemed preoccupied as he thoughtfully looked out of the window or silently played with his fingers, entwining them and then looking at his hands. I could see his unhappy expression, although he had negated my comments so contemptuously.

Once more, I broke the lengthy silence by conveying that perhaps I had touched on some painful feelings and he was not certain if he could trust me enough to talk about them. He looked directly at me and then down again. This encouraged me to suggest that, perhaps he was afraid that I might ask him to go like his mother did with his father or, his mother might tell him that she was fed up with his bed-wetting and ask him to leave like she did with his smelly father.

Initially, he just looked at me, but eventually I gathered that he had several fears. At times his mother did shout at him and he wondered if she would tell him to get out. He also related that he was worried about his mother. She worked too hard at the supermarket and when she was home, she spent all her time silently cleaning the house. He also felt that she should have tried harder to help his father instead of throwing him out. His Coke drinking and bed-wetting, he agreed, was to test his mother's patience. Would she get rid of him as he was becoming 'smelly' like his father? He knew she cried on the quiet and especially at night. Even though he felt angry towards her, he was also worried about her. After confiding that much, he seemed a lot calmer, looked directly at me and gave a fleeting smile before leaving.

As the therapy progressed, he never directly referred to his feelings about his father. Instead, he would indirectly refer to him with concern. For example, on one occasion he walked in, sat down and said, "Poor bugger! He will freeze to death out there."

To my enquiring look, he told me that he was referring to a homeless man he had seen on the way, sleeping in a doorway. After several unexpected little details like this, he began to share some feelings about his father and spoke more openly about how much he missed having him around. But he also felt that if he was around, he would dread his peers finding out the truth. Just as well he now kept away as no questions would be asked.

Once Ben could share his unhappy feelings with someone, his problems dramatically improved. He decided that the sugar in the Cokes he was drinking was not good for him. He personally did not enjoy diet Coke. He thought it tasted awful and by his fifteenth birthday, he had stopped drinking Coke altogether. His bed-wetting had stopped by then. His work at school improved and he started to participate in games and made a few friends. He infrequently saw his father, who was squatting with some others some distance away. Once, he despairingly confided that his father would never change. There was nothing anyone could do for him. Perhaps he would end up dying in the cold.

Some thoughts

These excerpts are an indication of how some feelings may be acted out as part of one's everyday behaviour when the mind is unable to cope with the reality. They demonstrate some intricate and involved psychic processes that had been acted out because they became unbearable for a young boy to tolerate the painful truth. It is common practise for adolescents, who are already trying to cope with the many changes connected with the vulnerable stage of moving from childhood to adulthood, to 'act out' their problems. Responsibilities hitherto avoided may feel burdensome and the connected feelings may be displayed to attract attention for help to sort out their problems. It takes some scope to understand what is going on in an adolescent's mind. It is recognised as one of the most difficult stages of human development, as explained in a later chapter.

As a young child, Ben could not comprehend the reality of his parents' painful situation. However, as an adolescent, he was torn between wanting a father around and simultaneously ashamed that his friends would know about his alcoholism. He was also desperately trying to understand what it was like to be his father. He could not share these thoughts with his mother. Caught up with her own feelings, or to avoid thinking about her own pain, she deliberately kept herself busy. She loved Ben and was perhaps over protective. He was too ashamed to speak about his feelings to any of his teachers at school. His way perhaps of giving meaning to what was happening to his father was to identify with him. Internalising the problem is one way of coping, but this does not help to heal the pain until the reality of the situation is accepted for what it represents. Only then peace of mind can be achieved. Often, the people closest to you are unable to help because they may also be involved from a different perspective.

Ben's mother was a vulnerable woman who also needed therapeutic support. Not only did she have to cope with an alcoholic partner, who was not around, but an adolescent son to whom she had to be both mother and father. She was understandably close to her son and was unable to see his pain for what it was. Obviously, Ben's father also needed help with his problem.

Adolescents often 'act out' their inner states in their outer behaviour. When feelings are displayed in a negative form, it is interpreted as irresponsible and unacceptable. This usually needs scrutiny before it may be understood as to why one is behaving in the manner one is doing. Once Ben's psychic defences had broken down, he became insightful and recognised that drinking large quantities of Coke secretly during the night and then wetting his bed was imitating and identifying with his alcoholic father. It was his only way of understanding his father's problem. Perhaps it was also a way of punishing his mother and undermining her authority, in that she is not so powerful in being able to be rid of 'smelly' people.

I also perceived in Ben some intense caring feelings towards his mother. He loved her, was concerned about her well-being. She worked too hard and hardly ever rested. During the therapy he realised how impossible it was for her to go on living with his father. To begin with, Ben replaced his real father with an imaginary one, himself. By drinking a litre of Coke and wetting the bed he identified with an alcoholic father. However, he could not simultaneously be the teenager he wanted to be at school, because of being ostracised for being smelly. He refused to continue seeing his father because of the shame he felt and being laughed at by his peer group.

The way individuals express their 'inner states' or feelings is remarkable. My understanding of Ben's simple statement that his father would die in the cold was perhaps true, but perhaps he also wished that his father would die and therefore disappear from their lives. It is not uncommon as an adolescent to wish that one's parents were different to the way they really are. Young people often phantasise about their relationships with a parent from all kinds of perspectives and have 'role models' to fill this need. For Ben, the stigma was too much to bear. He loved his father, but he could not accept him for who he was. At such a young and vulnerable stage, unfortunately, re-enactment through identification was his only way of expressing his real feelings.

Growing up as a normal teenager felt impossible with the stigma of an alcoholic, 'smelly' father. Fortunately, Ben did not surreptitiously start drinking alcohol like some teenagers do. His problems were recognised before he reached a stage of seriously imitating his father's alcoholism. The therapy supported him in understanding his inner troubled state, addressing his problems and alleviating some of the pain he had been experiencing. His personal life improved for the better as he made some friends, achieved at school and looked forward to going onto further education. As his therapy progressed I recognised another unconscious activity in Ben. He felt that his mother needed protection and in his phantasy he believed that he was her protector. He had begun to take on the pseudo role of the man of the house. This is not uncommon with young boys who have inadequate fathers – or vice versa with girls, if there is no strong motherly presence.

7

REMEMBRANCE OF THINGS PAST

Here Summer lingering, loiter I
When I with Summer, should be gone
Where only London lights the sky
I go and with me journeys "Swann"

Whose pages' dull laborious woof
Covers a warp of working times,
Of firelit nights beneath your roof
And sunlit days beneath your limes,

While, both at once and each in turn,
Sharp -tongued but smooth, like buttered knives,
We pared, with studied unconcern,
The problems of our private lives;

Those tiny problems, dense yet clear
Like ivory balls by Chinese craft

Pierced (where each hole absorbed a tear)
And rounded (where the assembly laughed).

Did all our laughter muffle pain,
Our candour simulate pretence?
Fear not. I shall not come again
To tease you with indifference.

Yet I may gaze for Oakham spire
Where London suns set, watery pale.
And dream, while tides of crimson fire
Sweep, smoking over Catmos vale.

C. K. Scott Moncrieff (1921)

The above poem was taken from the opening page of Scott Moncrieff's translation of Marcel Proust's novel, *A la Recherche du Temps Perdu* – which translates as *Remembrance of Things Past* or *In Search of Lost Time*. Moncrieff's poem conveys a double message. He is voicing his own feelings about longing to be in his own home, enjoying his lifestyle. But, this is intermingled with his work, which is to translate the feelings of Monsieur Charles Swann – a character in Proust's novel as Proust understood them. Moncrieff spent many, many hours absorbed in the world of the characters of Marcel Proust's lengthy novel. Published in the early twentieth century, the first two volumes are full of Proust's preoccupation with his observations and interpretations of what he assumes as Swann's thoughts and the people who attended the latter's social functions. Included in the novel are characteristic profiles and assumptions of the feelings of people he met at grand social events. The 3,000-page novel, published in seven volumes, is saturated with Proust's observations, feelings and interpretations he believed to be of those he associated or socialised with. Proust made an art of assuming he understood human behaviour. He had previously written several other novels before this lengthy one, which is now considered a masterpiece. It is one of the longest novels ever written. From a very young age, he suffered from asthmatic attacks and slept poorly. In his forties and suffering from insomnia, he spent long hours writing his remembrances in a cork-lined study to keep away the dust.

The writing of his pseudo-autobiographical novel began from the time he dipped a madeleine – a small cake and a special delicacy in parts of France – into a cup of lime blossom tea. This simple activity unexpectedly transported him emotionally to about the age of seven. The taste of the tea triggered off some early memories from his boyhood days. He drifted into a state of reverie, recalling and remembering the holidays he spent with his aunt, Tante Claire. She lived in a large house in a small town called D'Illiers, now also known as Combray, after the fictional name he had given it in his novel. During those long summer holidays, he frequently ate the little madeleine and drank lime blossom tea. Repeating an earlier activity transported him to some remembrances from his younger days. This unexpectedly cascaded into a flow of other connected memories and associations. For example, he recalled some nearby neighbours, whom he calls Monsieur Swann and his wife, regularly entertaining on a grand scale. He decided to write of these mental invasions as he recalled and remembered them.

One cannot know how much of what he wrote was from reality. It is now acknowledged to be a pseudo-autobiographical book, relating some of his life experiences as he remembered them from memory. Many of the characters resemble people he may have been friendly, acquainted or socialised with. As he came from an affluent background, it is possible that he socialised frequently with many of the upper circles and attended grand social functions of the privileged French society. During early childhood, due to asthma attacks he was given special attention by his mother which led to a distorted mother/child relationship.

The reader may wonder what this elaborate introduction regarding Proust has to do with the contents of this book. Simply, Proust was acting as a pseudo analyst, interpreting emotional or psychic activity. As mentioned earlier, his novel is saturated with what he believed to be the feelings of those he met or observed and how he interpreted them. He concluded that many of the people had secrets that led to lies and that they presented a 'false front'. He could be indirectly telling his own story because it is now understood that as an adult Proust was torn between heterosexuality and homosexuality. Perhaps Proust was telling us something about his own inner struggle, living at a time when homosexuality was not generally acceptable. He refers to 'the darkness we can never penetrate'. Given careful consideration I think that his hobby or interest, in observing, listening and interpreting, links with the basis of analytical work. The analyst tries to help the patient to understand the reality coming from the ego or 'inner state' instead of concentrating on the 'outer state' or super ego. Proust was a contemporary of Sigmund Freud (See Chapter11) a medical practitioner and methodical researcher, who established the mind as the source of conscious as well as 'unconscious processes'. Freud posited the concepts of the ego and the superego. Proust in long, elaborate, intricate and involved sentences describes that there is an 'I' and a 'me' self in every individual. In various, roundabout ways he describes the personality of most of his friends and acquaintances as functioning from the superficial 'me self' whilst ignoring what the 'I self' is telling them.

Throughout the several volumes of his novel he constantly presents his experiences as a stream of conscious remembrances of 'the truth'. For example, in his first volume, Proust conveys that as a young boy during his school days, if a book had been 'well-spoken of by the school master or a school friend, who, at that particular-time, seemed to me to be entrusted with the secret of the Truth and Beauty, things half felt by me, half incomprehensible, the full understanding of which was the vague but permanent objects of my thoughts. Next to this central belief, while I was reading, would be constantly in motion from my inner self to the outer world, towards the discovery of Truth.' In his novel, he constantly presents his experiences as a stream of conscious remembrances of past events, recalled from memory as the truth or that of others, they present as the truth. He is so carried away by some of what he recalls and remembers, interwoven with his current feelings, that the novel consists of some of the longest sentences ever written. This unfortunately hinders a wider readership. I think if he had chosen a style of writing perhaps similar to that of Emile Zola or Guy de Maupassant, more people would choose to read him. The first of the seven volumes, was published in 1913 and the last in 1927, five years after his death.

This chapter on Proust is also deliberately given for two further reasons. Firstly, I chose the title of his novel 'Remembrance of Things Past' as part of my book title, because I am writing about what my patients recalled and remembered from their past. All the reconstructed stories in Section One and the excerpts in this section are related to remembering the past. Secondly, Proust attempted to understand the true personality of others as well as himself, by observing, listening and interpreting, which basically and succinctly explains psychotherapeutic work. I think anyone who seriously wants to learn something about his personality and how it functions, can learn something by doing what Proust did, i.e. – listen to oneself and try to think about inner silent messages. However, like Proust they are also struggling inadequately and getting muddled with 'long, inexplicable, sentences' to solve what is troubling them.

This is when the expertise of the trained psychotherapist can clinically understand some of the complex and unfathomable thinking or behaviour and how it can be interpreted. There are people struggling to find answers for some of their unwanted, inexplicable feelings. They need clinical help not because they are stupid or inadequate but fail to understand the source of the problem coming from the unconscious, which requires a special understanding of emotional dysfunction. As explained in Section One, the secrets and lies that the people related to me in the consulting room were not assumed but were repeated from their experiences. The basis of clinical analytic work is to explore the feelings and thoughts to seek the 'truth', and to make the patient/client aware of what is being revealed or implied as a trained practitioner. Proust's awareness of seeking the truth is a common feature of psychotherapy, but not as a lay analyst. During clinical sessions, professionalism from a trained framework is adhered to. However, it may be argued that there is the patient's truth, the analyst's truth and 'the truth'. The patient may assume that some event happened that is far from what really occurred, or the analyst may have misunderstood the patient's statement. But professionalism requires an honest understanding wherein trust plays a very important role that develops as the therapy moves on.

Furthermore, another similarity with Proust's thinking lies in his references to remembering and recalling from childhood memory, which psychotherapists also do as explained below. These unexpected, unwanted, intrusive thoughts may give pleasure, or they may disturb our daily lives. But the major difference between Proust's stories and the ones given in these pages is that mine are from my clinical work experience and not as a lay analyst. Excerpts given to emphasise some of the activities of the personality are based on true stories. Remembering some disturbing feelings upsets one's equilibrium and often disrupts the lifestyle. Pleasurable feelings are also evoked but they enhance one's feelings by giving pleasure.

The following quotes from Proust do appropriately coincide with my thinking as a trained, clinical practitioner.

'The real voyage of discovery consists not in seeking new lands but new eyes.'

'If a little dreaming is dangerous, the cure for it is not to dream less but to dream more, to dream all the time.'

Through some stories of real life experiences, I have tried to clarify the statements and explanations given about the many facets of what we broadly acknowledge as 'our feelings'. These concepts are daily experienced by every normal functioning person as Proust was aware of. Without exception, good feelings are readily accepted. Disturbing feelings are often totally ignored, denied or paid very little attention to, until they begin to disturb one's lifestyle. As a keen philosopher, studying human behaviour from a personal and private stance, without his subjects being aware of his preoccupation, Proust could be thought of as a precursor to realistic, analytic work. But that is where the difference between his preoccupation and my clinical experience lies.

By sheer coincidence, my reading of *Remembrance of Things Past* was my holiday read during my long training as a psychoanalytic psychotherapist. However, it has only recently registered that some of the thoughts Proust was conveying, such as functioning from an 'I' or 'me' level, 'recalling and remembering' from childhood experiences are very closely related to my work. I facetiously now wonder how Marcel Proust, as a contemporary of Sigmund Freud, the pioneer of psychoanalysis, would have interpreted him or vice versa, had they met. Were they aware of each other's existence? Perhaps Proust had heard of Freud or perhaps Freud read Proust during his lifetime? Had they secretly tried to analyse each other? If they had met, would they have become the best of friends or would they have hated each other, with Freud thinking that Proust was a quack before offering to analyse him. On a more serious note, as discussed in more detail later, Freud was a professional medical scholar and a pioneer of psychoanalysis. He used a constructive methodology as a researcher with his hysterical patients. For Freud, it was not a self-indulgent pastime, as with Proust.

8

FEELINGS

Our daily lives are inundated with all kinds of feelings whether we want them or not. Many adults and especially young children, find it difficult to verbalise disturbing thoughts connected to those they love and believe love them in return. Feelings associated with happiness and well-being are readily enjoyed. Strange, disturbing, complicated, unwanted negative feelings often unbalance one's equilibrium, and can be detrimental to one's lifestyle. We hardly stop to think: *Where do our feelings originate from? Why do we have feelings? Why can't we control them and stop them from intruding upon our daily lives?* A very simple explanation for a complicated subject is that feelings stem from an intricate, innate process that is rooted in 'the senses' originating from a central part of the brain. Intense studies on the complexities of human behaviour connected to feelings exist, from anatomical, biological and emotional perspectives. Neurological scientists have located an area in our brain, the hypothalamus, which is a physiological part now commonly recognised and referred to as the mind, where our feelings originate from. The detailed information from those sources is necessary for those studying the subject. But the purpose of these pages is to give the reader some very simple examples of the different kinds of feelings we experience during our daily lives and how they impact on us.

Awareness of feelings was originally and seriously studied in the early twentieth century by the pioneer of psychoanalysis, Sigmund Freud (1). As a psychiatrist, working with institutionalised patients, he decided to treat some of the hysterical female patients with a more humane form of treatment instead of the harsh methods in practice. He encouraged them to talk to him about their various ailments whilst he listened and keenly observed them. He made scrupulous notes soon after a session of what the patient conveyed and his observations. As their trust in him grew, he realised they were sharing some of their very disturbing thoughts connected to desires, phantasies and experiences, which they could not speak about to anyone else. Some of them claimed that they recalled and remembered being sexually abused or having prohibited sexual desires towards a close member of the family. Since Freud had written about this very early work, some of the stories related by these women have been thought of as hysterical, distorted versions. Whether they were phantasies or the truth, these intrusive feelings and thoughts caused these women to be hysterical and disturbed their mental well-being. By being able to talk to someone about their feelings, who sympathetically listened, without being accusative or critical, helped them to feel alleviated.

Since Freud inaugurated the practice of psychoanalysis, the basis of psychotherapeutic intervention is about helping the patient/ client to understand as much as possible the source of his disturbing feelings. Our multifaceted psyche or 'inner world' is not altogether as mysterious as one may imagine and can be understood if desired. Disturbing, unfathomable feelings often cause unhappiness, anxiety, stress or even depression to a varying degree. With the knowledge of learned theory as well as undergoing many years of analysis, (see Chapter 11) the psychotherapist, in practise, discovers and understands a fair amount of the complexities of the patient's inner life through listening and observing.

As earlier stated the intention of this book is to create some awareness of how psychotherapeutic intervention helps people with their emotional problems. Most people do not hesitate to see the G.P. for physical discomfort. Perhaps, the thought of having to pay for psychotherapy could be one reason for not wanting to seek help. Many are not aware that psychotherapy is available in the NHS. Nevertheless, a fair amount of fear and/or scepticism still prevails. Psychotherapeutic intervention is not a mystical practice nor a form of witchcraft. It is a humane person-centred activity wherein trust and empathy facilitates an environment to speak freely of disturbing feelings.

Before Freud's intense study and recognition of the unconscious, an awareness of the various forms of feelings was expressed through the medium of art. Shakespeare was not only a talented writer; he also had an intuitive grasp of emotionality. The late Bernard Levin, journalist and critic, adeptly wrote an unnamed poem on Shakespeare's vast knowledge on feelings and the behaviour of mankind. Levin succinctly expresses that every form of emotion one can think of has been written about in one of Shakespeare's plays: love, joy, jealousy, envy, lust, hate, lies, anger, sadness, grief, remorse, mourning and melancholia are, consciously or unconsciously, portrayed by his characters. Currently, it is not uncommon for quotes from his plays to be used as examples in psychoanalytic literature. Over the centuries poets have similarly expressed their feelings through their poems. William Blake was observant and insightful of psychological issues. Through his poems in 'Songs of Innocence and of Experience' he was an exponent of the detrimental treatment of children.

Music stirs up all kinds of feelings in us. From ancient times, it has played a significant role as part of every culture, to express emotionality. There are songs for celebratory occasions like births, puberty and weddings, as well as appropriate ones for funerals and mourning. Musical composers express their feelings through their work. Opera, a form of musical art, is becoming more popular to a wider audience through the media. I think many opera goers identify with the performing artists and the music, as they see a connection with some of their own feelings. Even without understanding the words when sung in another language, one is sensitive to the various feelings conveyed.

Several composers expressed their feelings of joy or sadness through their music. Some had a difficult childhood and perhaps found relief through their musical compositions. Wagner, I particularly feel, left us a legacy of some of the most exquisite, soul-searching music. If one can overlook Wagner's atrocious anti-Semitic thinking, one discovers someone who was aware of in-depth feelings, as Shakespeare was. In his 'Ring Cycle', comprised of four operas lasting approximately fifteen hours, he makes many people experience almost every emotion imaginable. His music influences and penetrates many listener's sensitivity, transporting the individual through realms of varied feelings.

When young people, especially adolescents, behave in a manner that parents or someone in authority may find difficult to cope with, they may react insensitively. At times they may verbalise their own fears and anxious feelings either threateningly, insensitively or in a playful manner. This may later result in an unforeseen scenario. During my work as a clinician, I discovered that some clients' problems were rooted from some such remark made by a parental figure in the past. The following is an example of a remark, unintentionally made and how it reacted on the daughter. The mother doubtlessly loved her daughter.

* * *

Indra was an attractive, intelligent, lively young Asian woman. She was the first generation of her family to be born in Britain. Her parents, who were of a similar background and ethnicity, came to the UK as students, met here and married. Indra was the only daughter, with two older brothers but she was neither spoilt nor conceited. She came over as a considerate, sincere and likeable person. She had a very creative and lucrative job and was dating a colleague, James, and they led a hectic social life. She was referred because of her recent bereavement. Her mother had been ill with a chronic heart condition for some time. Her death was not entirely unexpected, but the family were shocked to see how Indra's personality had completely altered soon after her mother's death.

She became introverted, morose, silent, and refused to go to work after the normal period of mourning. She spent solitary, long hours in her room. After much persuasion, she reluctantly came out for meals, but didn't eat properly. She lost weight and became slovenly. Previously she had been very particular about her appearance. Her father was distraught with worry and felt helpless. Indra also refused to see James and none of her family could persuade her to shift out of her low mood. Almost six months after her mother's death, her second brother, whom she was closest to, persuaded her to see the GP, who referred her to me.

For weeks she remained almost silent and only answered briefly to anything I said. Nevertheless, she continued to come regularly and gradually became a little more responsive. She launched on trivial subjects and evaded anything to do with her personal feelings. At times I felt desperately inadequate and realised she was transferring some of her despair onto me. At one meeting she said something to the effect that her home life was now very different to how it used to be. I tentatively suggested that the absence of her mother had obviously changed the family situation. She bluntly and coldly responded, "We all knew it was going to happen. She lived for longer than we expected. She was lucky to reach her sixties."

Indra sounded cold and unfeeling. She remained expressionless. Her sessions continued in this manner for some weeks. She was unresponsive and detached. I once alluded to her icy feelings towards me adding that perhaps I reminded her of her mother. She was afraid to share her thoughts with me. I might let her down like her mother and disappear. She was immediately on the defensive, criticising me of being 'a know-all'.

Another long silence followed before she shifted around as if she was uncomfortable, which made me realise I had intuitively touched on something significant. I repeated that I understood how much the loss of her mother must mean to her. But her mother would not want her to be in the state she was in now. She would have preferred for Indra to be the person she used to be so proud of.

The tears started to come with some heavy breathing, as if she was gasping for breath. She curled up and half turned away from me. Eventually, between pauses and gasping, she related, "When I was at secondary school, a group of us usually hung around together at the weekends. My father was often away on business during those years. He started to work more from home after I left to go to university. Perhaps he thought I was always there to keep her company."

There was a long pause before she continued, "She was reluctant to let me go out in the evenings. My older brothers were usually out with their friends. My mother often started off by refusing to let me go out. She said that my dad would not approve, but I always managed to persuade her to agree and returned in good time, as I had promised."

There was another long pause and more tears, before she finally continued, "I often lied about what we did. I used to tell my mother that we stayed at one of my friend's homes, had snacks and watched a DVD. I lied and lied. We often went into the city centre or to the cinema with the boys. Sometimes, we went to the park and messed around. She would never have allowed me to go if she had known the truth." She burst out crying. When she calmed down a little she volunteered between sobs, "Nearly always after she gave me permission, she used to say, 'What will your father say? You will be the death of me.'"

Some thoughts

That repeated expression from her mother, "You will be the death of me", combined with the guilt of lying, made Indra feel she had brought about her mother's death prematurely. She had internalised what her mother had said. The fact that her mother had survived her heart condition for longer than expected became immaterial. Perhaps Indra's lying brought upon guilt feelings as she will never be able to confess the truth to her mother. A further interpretation may be that her mother colluded with her by not telling her father the truth. The shock of losing her mother persuaded her that she was the cause of her mother's death and that she ought to be punished. Expected or not the death of her mother whom she loved was obviously devastating. Indra was a very intelligent person, but her feelings of guilt connected with the lies dominated her inner state. By isolating and almost starving herself, she would also die. She felt that she did not deserve to lead a contented and successful life. She was unable to mourn because of her lies. She felt that she did not deserve to be happy. It was now too late to make amends and tell her mother the truth.

Indra was in a state of melancholia and could not mourn her mother's death. Her punishment to deprive herself of a life of her own felt like a re-enactment of her mother's life. Her mother had been a graduate who worked until she had her eldest son. She had never gone back to work. She sacrificed her career to bring up three children and then the heart condition was diagnosed. Her mother may have unwittingly referred to this, perhaps without realising it. There may also have been some unspoken feelings of resentment on the mother's part regarding the freedom her daughter enjoyed, whilst she felt trapped like a prisoner at home.

Once Indra started to talk about some of her innermost fears and difficulties, her health and mental well-being improved. By the anniversary of her mother's death, she had mourned her loss and became more of her old self again. She went back to work and the relationship with James resumed but in a less hectic manner. He had been very patient with her and was well liked by her father and the rest of the family. Perhaps her refusal to see James was 'acting out' the feelings she assumed her mother had experienced when her father was often away from home. Indra was naturally devastated by the loss of her mother, but certain factors prevented her from grieving. She felt guilty about telling her mother lies and then it became too late to tell the truth. I oscillated from being the good mother whom she could confide in and at other times she was not going to tell me what she was doing secretly.

The following pages introduce the various kinds of feelings in a simplified form, avoiding psychoanalytic jargon as much as possible.

Positive or good, happy feelings

Positive feelings are easier to cope with because they are associated with pleasure. They may be anticipated, widely acknowledged, looked forward to and welcomed. Positive thinking can instigate similar feelings in others. This can lead to promoting a better understanding with family and friends. Happy feelings in connection with celebrations, spread joy around. Everyone generally accepts positive feelings spontaneously without questioning. Intellectual achievement also brings on feelings of joy. Very rarely does one pause to question why one is feeling happy.

There are many remarkable people who are born with physical deficiencies, or a hereditary condition through no fault on their part. Many however adjust in a positive manner and in admirable ways. Some have bequeathed us with their knowledge and skills in various forms unimaginable by 'normal people'. For example, Louis Braille, blind from the age of three, devised what is now commonly known as Braille to help the blind to read. Another example is Stephen Hawkins, the physicist. The list is endless of past and contemporary people who have accepted their unfortunate disabilities and have cultivated positive thinking.

Negative feelings

Some extraordinary people have tolerated and worked through most difficult and unimaginable situations by adjusting their negative experiences to think positively, instead of harbouring negative thoughts. Through reconciliation, they survive and continue to live fruitful lives. Nelson Mandela is an excellent example in not harbouring negative feelings towards his persecutors. His experiences were of the extreme kind. Enduring such harsh treatment over so many years required an extraordinary form of mental frame work. However, his story indicates that unwanted and undesired feelings that cause pain, could be accepted for what they represent and negotiated. One can never be rid of unwelcome, undesirable negative experiences because they remain in the 'inner self' as 'unconscious processes'. Learning to live with those unwelcome feelings is the only way to achieve peace of mind. They are part of the personality and should be accepted as one's life experiences, before peace of mind can be achieved.

Adults who continually experience violence from others or children who are abused emotionally, physically and sexually have no means of defending themselves. The horrendous treatment and undermining leaves them feeling defenceless and emotionally disturbed. Many such cases need professional expertise to help them adjust mentally. This is never an easy task to achieve because the associated pain also returns and may be too unbearable. Some people who have been physically or emotionally violated by loved ones, may internalise their negative feelings as benign anger. There are people who become actively violent and destructive and want to hurt others as much as they feel hurt. Pseudo-power as a front is another form of hiding or ignoring real feelings of pain. Many bullies and bossy people present a form of power over others to countermand internal feelings of weakness. This kind of destructiveness eventually begets destructiveness to the self. At times the 'inner hurt' is displayed in some strange negative behaviour, common amongst adolescents, notorious for vandalism. The revengeful act may not always be directed to the real perpetrator.

Resentful, suppressed feelings connected to negative experiences from younger days may become activated later, during adulthood, in strange ways. Resurgence may occur when something connected from those days reminds one of the past. The person may not always realise the connection. Unexpectedly, those well-hidden feelings are 'acted out'. They may uncontrollably be directed towards another at any moment. The following vignette is about someone who unusually and unexpectedly displayed negative behaviour. This was directed towards another worker who became the target for his benign anger.

* * *

Kris was a fifty-year-old skilled worker with good job prospects; he earned well and lived in a large house with his wife and two grown-up children. He led a very satisfactory lifestyle, played an active role in the community and was highly respected. He unexpectedly received a Christmas card from his only sibling, a younger brother who had gone abroad. The brothers had not met or kept in touch for many years. The card conveyed that he was thinking about visiting with his wife and daughter in the summer. He wanted to see their mother, who was now very old and in a nursing home. Soon after the news, Kris became ill, began to suffer from violent headaches and became irritable. Things came to a peak when he angrily hurled a tool at a co-worker. Fortunately, no one was hurt. He was sent home on leave and told to sort out his problem.

After some persuasion by his wife, he came to see me. As usual it took some months before he felt able to speak about the real problem, which was to do with his brother.

"I dread his coming. He was a philanderer. My parents always spoilt him. He was their favourite. He twisted them around his little finger. They believed everything he said. He was a womaniser and treated many badly and yet the girls fell for him. He has obviously changed. I never thought he would marry and settle down. I still think of him as he used to be." He fidgeted and looked a little uncomfortable. "After my father died, we moved into the big house with my mother." He paused and fidgeted with his glasses. I felt he was being evasive.

I repeated, "Moved into the big house."

"Yes! Our little flat had become too cramped for the four of us. The children, as teenagers, needed a room each." Another pause before he continued, "It seemed the best thing to do all round. My mother was getting old and she needed help as the house was too big for her to maintain. I knew my mother was also feeling lonely, although she would never admit to that. Two years ago, she decided to go into the nursing home. It was for the best as she never got on with my wife. Both wanted to be 'mistress of the house'. They were always at loggerheads about everything." He sighed. "When my mother got into one of her moods, she would go off to her sisters for several days without informing us. The first time this happened we were worried but soon found out that she was with my aunt who phoned to let us know. She was as surprised as we were. This became a pattern with my mother whenever she disagreed with my wife. She reappeared as suddenly as she went off." He paused for a long time before continuing.

"One day she suddenly announced that she wanted to go into a private home that was not too far from us. She decided that she needed assistance as her arthritis had worsened. I think she was pleased to get away and have the company of her own age group."

Kris continued to talk about his mother for several further sessions. Then, one day, he arrived looking alarmed and nervous. He had received a letter from his brother confirming their flight details. The brother's coming now felt inevitably imminent. He looked anxious and between several pauses, he said, "My mother had to sign some papers before going into the nursing home. My father had left the house and all the contents to her." Another long pause before he continued hesitantly, "It was still her house. I had a will made when she was moving into the nursing home, which I included with all the papers she had to sign. My mother trusted me, believing all the papers had to do with moving into the home. She did not question me and signed the various forms. A young nurse acted as a witness and trustingly signed without reading the various forms. I did not tell her specifically about the will."

He stopped to wipe his glasses. I could see he was tearful. Softly, he disclosed, "I completely left out my brother. I know my mother would like everything shared between us. He was her favourite regardless of his neglectful behaviour towards her. I know I should have consulted her. I felt it my right to inherit all. My brother had deserted her. He used to phone her from various places and then it was just a card on her birthday or for Christmas."

He sighed several times and became emotional. After another lengthy silence he hesitantly confessed, "It's making me sick. I told my wife what I had done. She was initially shocked but calmly told me to destroy it and bring up the subject with my mother and brother when he comes. My mother is still very alert and will know exactly what she wants to do with the property and the contents." After a brief pause, shaking his head, he volunteered, "I am not a dishonest person. I am the trustee of my local club and am very particular about handling the money, I make sure the secretary double checks the banking."

Some thoughts

Kris's negative feeling towards his irresponsible brother, who had been favoured by his parents, stirred up some past envious and angry feelings. Contrary to his usual likeable, helpful nature, he acted uncharacteristically. He had been in denial until his brother made himself known again. The suppressed, benign anger became activated and he lost control. He 'acted out' this anger uncontrollably towards another. During the therapy Kris was able to think about those long stored revengeful feelings. When recalled he could understand and make connections with his current behaviour. He had never been aware or able to think he harboured such feelings against his brother.

After the display of uncontrollable anger he was in a state of shock. He somatised his feelings, which were physically developed to having headaches and other minor illnesses. He could see his wrongdoing for what it really represented. He confessed to being angry, a feeling that went back to their adolescent days. He confessed to being envious of his brother. Although he was the good, caring and respectful son, he had always been overlooked by his parents in preference to the irresponsible, spoilt brother. Internally, Kris carried a grudge against his brother and unconsciously he acted revengefully. It was his way of getting back at him.

Disowning and transferring feelings

Some feelings make one feel uncomfortable. Rather than think sincerely why one is having those feelings, they may be disowned and transferred as that of another. This kind of functioning is an unconscious, mental process known as projection. They are usually of an undesirable nature and painful to contemplate. Those feelings are often transferred as that of someone close, like a parent, partner, colleague or the analyst. I repeat that this kind of behaviour is unconscious. The perpetrator is not consciously aware of what he/she is doing. If this kind of activity is continually directed towards the same person, the vulnerable recipient believes or thinks it is his/her characteristic. The psychotherapist is trained to detect such behaviour, theoretically known as 'projective identification', a concept originally introduced by Melanie Klein (3). It is a powerful and intricate mental or psychic activity. Simply, one is being brainwashed by another without either being consciously aware of what is happening.

Transference of unwanted feelings of one's undesirable self or projective identification is a common feature amongst adolescents. They easily persuade another that an unwanted, undesired feeling is that of that person. With adults the projection is often directed toward someone who is less assertive and tolerant. Unfortunately, the recipient is being made a scapegoat without realising it. This kind of emotional activity is common between couples and other couplings. The following example is of someone who came for psychotherapy when his wife threatened to leave him.

* * *

Some powerful transference feelings in projective identification with his partner were noted in Adrian, a thirty-six-year-old. He was an intelligent professional and married with two young children. His continual criticisms and temper tantrums were directed towards his wife, Sue. He would suddenly, for no given reason, find some fault or other. He would suggest that she was ignorant, dressed slovenly or compared her to some other woman who was the ideal woman. At first Sue alternated with believing, doubting or ignoring his behaviour. Then she realised that Adrian's continual undermining had something to do with himself. She had been successful during her working life, and often admired by colleagues for her quick thinking and intelligence. She then started to challenge or retaliate. Adrian started drinking a lot more than usual. After a few drinks he raised his voice and would approach her threateningly. One evening the children heard the row and came downstairs crying. Sue had had enough. She put the children into the car, said she was going to her parents and wanted a divorce.

At the beginning of his therapy he spent many a session criticising almost everyone he knew. He loved Sue, but she often irritated him with her stupid chatter and he grew impatient with her. He continually undermined her as useless, simple minded and unsophisticated. Soon after he would contradict all this adding that she was a caring wife and mother. Intermittently, I gathered through his sessions that she was an intelligent woman who had temporarily given up her successful career to bring up their two children. She came from a large family and mothering came naturally to her. I felt that he was conveying an undercurrent of envy.

Adrian had been adopted by an aunt and her husband, who had one son, a couple of years older than him. He had lost his parents when he was about four. He vaguely gathered that they died within months of each other – his mother first, followed by his father. The aunt once said that they had led a reckless lifestyle. He also related that he loved his aunt and uncle and they were the only parents he knew. He was also very close to his cousin.

At the time he was seeing me he was struggling to finish writing a research paper. With two young children around, he did not get much time during the weekends to concentrate on the paper. All this sounded plausible and realistic, but I noted that many of the quarrels he related originated from Sue's inefficiency.

At one session he said, "She annoys me when she makes stupid grammatical mistakes. It is difficult to have a decent conversation with her."

After such critical anecdotes of Sue, Adrian always ended by saying that she was a good, caring and loving mother.

Once he walked into a session looking angry and did not greet me. He slumped onto the couch and remained silent for some time. I commented on him being very angry, which he seemed reluctant to share today. Insultingly, he replied that I thought I knew everything, adding, "Why do you presume I am angry? What if I am feeling angry? Why shouldn't I feel the way I do? You sound just like Sue!"

Eventually I gathered that he did not get the promotion he was expecting. It was given to another colleague whom he criticised as being stupid. "I am as good as him, if not better! It was definite favouritism. Totally unfair and I'm going to take it up with the senior directors."

He blamed his failure on Sue not being able to help him by giving him some space to get on with his research. She could have taken the children to her parents at the weekends. He admitted at a later session that this was not true. He also related that Sue was earning as much as he was since recently taking on some work she does from home while the children are at school. This made him feel even more inadequate. He was transferring and disowning his inadequacy to Sue and his colleague.

Some thoughts

Thereafter it took Adrian some time to realise that it was his personality that prevented him from achieving his goals. He was egotistical and thought himself superior to others and especially Sue. Perhaps these feelings were connected to losing his parents at such a vulnerable age and not feeling adequate to do anything about that. His feelings of hopelessness made him project them as that of others and especially Sue. It took some time before he would accept these interpretations. Eventually, he disclosed that Sue had been very successful and popular at her workplace. His feelings oscillated between admiration and hate. During the latter times, he disowned his inadequate feelings as that of hers. Adrian was envious of Sue.

Envy is an inner state of being. It is pervasive without the person being consciously aware of his/her state of mind, disowning undesirable characteristics as that of another. The perpetrator usually targets someone who is vulnerable and can be easily persuaded. The subject is not consciously aware of what he/she is doing. It is such a subtle mental mechanism that it is not easy for the object to recognise what is happening as it is an unconscious process. It differs from jealousy, when the subject consciously desires to possess something another has. One knowingly is jealous of someone's looks, intellect or possession. Jealousy and envy are often thought of as being the same or very similar. It was Melanie Klein who noted the difference, as she recognised these features during her work with infants and children.

Feelings stirred up through listening to another

A long, forgotten experience of one's own may be stirred up and recalled during communication with another. During therapy, 'the stirring up of feelings' in the other/therapist is referred to as the 'countertransference', an expression usually confined to the analytic world. Analysts are no exception. They can also easily be influenced by what the client is conveying, However, their training usually comes to the rescue. They learn to adopt a frame of mind during their clinical work to recognise and refrain from colluding with the patient. It is important to separate the patient's thoughts and feelings from one's own personal thoughts. Professional etiquette is to never exploit the patient with one's intrusive and negative feelings. Such thoughts should be left until later to be discussed during their own analysis, supervision or thought about privately. Collusion with the patient is detrimental to the therapeutic treatment.

Countertransference may also be seen from a positive perspective. The analyst may have undergone a similar experience as that of a patient. Although, this might be very difficult if it is related to something painful, the analyst will have a better understanding of what the experience involves and be helpful to the client. An insightful, appropriate and understanding interpretation could result in positive relief for the patient. The analyst, however, should under no circumstances confuse her personal experience with that of the patient as this will be detrimental and counter productive to the therapeutic treatment. She should continually be aware and differentiate what is coming from the patient to that of her own experience.

Summary

Widely recognised and accepted in the psychotherapeutic circle is that there is a powerful need in the patient to continue to externalise those troublesome internal states of mind outside the sessions and especially during the break from therapy. 'Acting out' often continues in relation to others until the next session. Psychotherapy makes the individual feel needy and vulnerable whilst working through some experiences related to childhood problems. Without cognitively being aware of this the patient may regress to that earlier stage of his lifespan. Although in the outer world the individual carries on as normal, feelings of dependency may get emotionally stirred up. The vulnerable child part craves for some nurturing. It is accepted by professionals and patients that some 'acting out' is part of the treatment before a balanced state of mind can be achieved.

Clinical work acknowledges positive feelings, but it is often more centred on the negative aspects of the personality. Psychotherapeutic intervention is about working through and integrating past negative experiences and the feelings connected with them. During therapy one learns to accept them as part of the personality. They are then tolerated from a different perspective. Acceptance of the 'truth' is required before any healing can take place. This may involve feelings of remorse, guilt, anger or pain before a healthy mind and emotional well-being may be achieved.

9

MEMORY

What does the word memory mean? We understand that it is a facility that helps us to recall and remember from the past. We also accept that memory plays a significant role during our daily lives. We have some control over our memory but not totally. Most of our past activities, experiences or learned knowledge, return with or without prompting, whilst others may be totally forgotten without us actively trying to do that. Remembrance of things past from memory, irrespective of cultural background, traditions or social values is a universal human activity. Memory is therefore linked with remembrance of past activities during the present and remains within us for the future. As T.S. Eliot eloquently reminded us that our, 'present and time past, are both perhaps present in time future', further clarifying, that 'time future' is 'contained in time past'. Wilfred Bion (4) a psychoanalyst similarly conveyed that, 'The invariants in an event which is unconscious because obscured by memory, *although* it has happened can disclose itself in the future. Memory and desire may be regarded as past and future senses'. Memory can therefore be considered as timeless. As earlier explained, we now generally accept that as human beings we function from both a conscious and an unconscious level. All our experiences from as far back as childhood, are stored as 'unconscious processes'. With this concept in mind, I will try to briefly explain the functioning of an intricate faculty that we recognise as 'memory' from a psychotherapeutic paradigm.

We have very little or no choice as to what we recall and remember from memory. We can voluntarily prompt our memory to recall learned knowledge and some experiences, both good and bad. There is no assurance that this could always be achieved for several reasons as explained later. However, complex processes of satisfying instinctual needs – like hunger, quenching thirst and other bodily requirements – are activated involuntarily through the 'senses'. These impulses automatically come from memory, stored within the complexity of the mind as survival is a basic instinct. Simultaneously, the mind is like a hidden camera we have no control over, constantly taking snapshots or slides of our other sensual activities. These images are stored and cannot be easily discarded or destroyed, except in exceptional cases when one becomes traumatised.

Psychotherapists and Child Development Psychologists recognise that every experience from a very young age is imprinted on the mind and later recalled through memory. Most of what we learn either intellectually or from experience remain as 'explicit' memory whilst others become 'implicit'. Detrimental and traumatic activities towards an individual during childhood, involving harmful, horrific scenarios, may become distorted and stored as 'implicit memory', if not altogether 'blocked off' or permanently erased. A vulnerable child is unable to process repeated, horrific experiences.

Eschewing Freud's concept or not, of 'unconscious processes', we continually recall and remember past events either willingly or recall without making a conscious effort. Unfortunately, there are times when one has no choice as to what the memory may bring to the conscious level. A realistic solution is to accept the past unsavoury, unwanted experiences, acknowledge them for what they represent as part of one's personality. This is often no easy task as one requires a framework of mind to tolerate the associated emotional pain and discomfort associated with the remembrance (as conveyed in Section One). The psychotherapist can often help to disentangle some of the disturbing thoughts. I say some, because as previously mentioned 'implicit memory' can play a part in obstructing the truth. There are times when one is not aware of why or what is causing the distress even though one is being as honest with oneself as possible. In other circumstances, trying to forget or ignore unwanted feelings is only a temporary solution because past experiences can never be rid of and they will resurface at any time. Obviously, they need to be understood for what they represent before they can be accepted as part of the personality. During a therapy session, a clue coming from the patient, may give the analyst an opportunity to encourage the patient to 'free associate', which might activate the memory further. Some of the remembrances may be 'explicit' but one should bear in mind that some of it could be 'implicit'.

For some people, the consequences of having recalled from memory, with all its pain and distress, may productively be transformed to creativity. An example of this as mentioned earlier is Marcel Proust. It may be argued that he was phantasising and that it is only a novel, coming from someone's imagination. One will never know for certain. I think it was Proust's way of trying to come to terms with some of his own personal difficulties and wanting to confront the 'truth' from his 'I' self. Perhaps he realised that he was functioning from a 'me' self because he could not tell others the 'explicit' truth.

Many people spend most of their lifetime concentrating on achievement rather than being. Much of our lifestyle today is inundated with electronic devices and other distractions. This to some extent has replaced our initiative to be creative. From an alternate viewpoint, one must not lose sight of the fact that these devices are the result of a few people's innate, aesthetic, creative experiences, stirred up from inexplicable, in-depth feelings.

False Memory

Early on, when the developing mind/psyche is at a vulnerable stage and dependent on others, the young mind may not be able to defend itself by processing negative experiences. The child has no choice but to repress those painful feelings. Emotional damage experienced at that stage may later be recalled with feelings of despair, vengeance, or are so painful that they may cause mental disturbances. To accept the real experience in its true form will necessitate further emotional processing before some peace of mind may be achieved. In extreme cases when the damage had been of a serious nature, the person may acquire a 'false memory' of those past experiences. Even professional support may not be able to help with some such cases. Some suffer from severe depression, become mentally ill or traumatised.

During psychotherapeutic intervention, it has been known that some recollections that may seem explicit have been distorted versions through confusion or avoidance of the connected pain. One should not assume that all or any memory of childhood or at any stage of the lifespan is unquestionably the truth. Experiences of unpleasant, physically violating and painful or emotionally unbearable may be annihilated. Sexual and physical abuse, a topical feature, is often too painful an experience for the vulnerable mind to negotiate. To understand what is happening at the time may be beyond the comprehension of a young child. Shock may create uncertainty and confusion, especially when a member of the family, who is supposed to be kind and loving, becomes nasty and hurtful. The painful experience is denied, completely blocked off or becomes implicit. Some years later, during puberty, adolescence, adulthood, or in later life, another associated experience may trigger off uncomfortable feelings that are partly connected to the dissociated past.

A deprived child may adopt the personality of another as a means of denying and mentally avoiding the real pain. Negative experiences may result in accusing another innocent person, resembling the culprit because of the belief that closely loved ones could not be so hurtful. The false memory syndrome may be connected to inaccurate timescales and facts. As previously mentioned, feelings are transient and therefore difficult to always pinpoint. The imagery of repressed feelings may be inaccurate, fragmented and partially true. There is undoubtedly truth in the saying 'there is no smoke without fire', but can one always be certain as to whom or what started the fire? Contributors who have studied the 'false memory syndrome' or 'false beliefs' convey that something definitively happened during childhood, referring to the distorted accounts as 'false positives'. Alternatively, there are adults who have totally suppressed and dissociated themselves from an early experience, falsely believing that it did not happen. This is technically understood as 'false negatives'. Both aspects, whether in a state of confusion or denial, stem from unavoidable feelings rooted in the memory. The 'false memory syndrome', whether 'false positive' or 'false negative', can be evoked during any stage of the lifespan. Many eventually accept the inner pain, but others are unable to do so. Emotionally agonising experiences may be 'acted out' in various ways like the example given below.

* * *

A very angry fifteen-year-old, who was continuously violent and disruptive, vandalised a waiting area in a clinic and had to be placed into temporary care. He attempted to run away from the care home several times. He related that he did not want to stay in the care home because his key worker was sexually abusing him during the night. It took some time before it was discovered that he was traumatised. He falsely accused the female key worker. After giving a fair amount of thought it was recognised that he was in a state of a 'false positive' mind. On no account could the key worker have done this. She had never been in the care home at night. During the day, she always spent time with a small group that included him. Initially, she saw him a few times with his mother in the presence of a social worker. During those times, he never said a word but rocked forward and backwards, looking at the floor. Furthermore, the key worker lived with her husband and her children, a distance away. Much later, in therapy he admitted that he had been sexually abused since the age of eleven by his alcoholic mother. He acted out his angry feelings towards another, rather than the real culprit. He was emotionally hurt by his mother's activities, but he also wanted to protect her, so became psychically split. He needed to expose the maltreatment and hurt he suffered but could only do this through being 'false positive'.

Trauma

Severe destructive incidents affect one's tranquillity and people are often traumatised. Authorities on the subject have written about the consequences of these disasters and how they could be helped. During everyday life experiences people and especially children may feel mildly traumatised through some personal experience. Externally, many such people lead what are considered as normal, successful lifestyles. Some associated incident during a later stage may make them behave in an unexpected manner because of the connection with the earlier, traumatic experience.

* * *

Jane, an attractive, seventeen-year-old, and her childhood friend, Dan, were inseparable. They met when she was about five at primary school, became childhood sweethearts and did most things together, until they moved on to further education. They attended different sixth form colleges. Jane became friendly with Tina, who was studying the same subjects. If Jane was not with Dan, she was with Tina, who lived in another district, a bus ride away. During that first year, just before the Christmas break, Tina was participating in a college concert. Jane was invited to it and she asked Dan to accompany her. After the concert, Jane introduced Tina to Dan. From there on, all three occasionally went out together. She noticed that Dan and Tina often teased one another. At times, she felt left out and jealous. Not long after the Christmas holidays, she noticed that Dan was not as keen on going out. He protested that he needed to get on with his studies to get good grades, to get a place at the university he was keen on. She felt left out and neglected. Feeling frustrated and fed up one Saturday afternoon, Jane turned up unexpectedly at Tina's to be told that she was upstairs in her bedroom. To Jane's horror, she related that she found Dan in bed with Tina. Shocked, she ran down the stairs and fainted. Tina's mother, hearing the commotion, found her, pale and semi-conscious. The mother was aware of Tina and Ian running down the stairs and Ian rushing out, slamming the front door. Tina protested that it was not Dan when Jane accused her of having an affair with him. All Tina's pleas were ignored. Jane walked out. Tina's mother was too shocked and distressed about her daughter and refused to say anymore to Jane.

Tina repeatedly said that Dan had never come to her home. Ian was an old school friend of hers, but Jane could not recall Tina previously mentioning him. Tina explained that Ian was scared of her mother, so had bolted out. She offered to introduce Ian, but Jane decided she did not want to have anything more to do with Tina. When Dan was confronted by Jane about the incident, he was shocked and could not persuade her that he had never been to Tina's house. He was studying as he had said. From there on, Tina and Jane's friendship ended and after college, they never ever saw each other again. Jane vaguely heard that Tina had gone abroad for her gap year. Several years later, Dan and Jane married. Although the incident had long been forgotten by both, it remained traumatised in Jane.

In her mid-thirties Jane saw me for psychotherapy concerning some other reasons. Jane was a very sensitive, serious person and often felt insecure. During a session nearing Christmas, she spoke about an office party she had gone to with Dan. She thought that Dan was over-friendly with some of his female colleagues. She could not pinpoint anything that stirred up her jealous feelings. From some of her previous comments, I gathered Dan to be an overtly friendly person. It was at this stage that she recalled the incident with Tina from her teenage days. She believed that the scenario she had witnessed was the explicit truth. She had forgiven Dan a long time ago and it was never mentioned again. She had totally forgotten the incident until it surfaced at this stage, nearing Christmas time.

Several questions come to mind. Did Jane really witness what she claimed to have seen? Was Tina with Ian or Dan? Was Dan telling the truth? Perhaps, Jane was very angry with Dan for ignoring her while he was seriously studying. I think the temporary loss of Dan's companionship had stirred up some childhood thoughts of loss and desertion. She had previously conveyed that when she was about five, she recalls her parents often quarrelling. One day she was in her room upstairs when she heard the front door slam. She looked out of the window to see her father walk out the front gate. She called out to him. He did not turn around or look up. At the time she thought he was going out as he usually did after a quarrel. She never saw him again. This was a traumatic experience for a vulnerable child. People who ignored her presence, walked away from her life and never returned. Dan had excluded her, so was never going to come back.

This early childhood experience of someone she loved disappearing from her life without an explanation, clearly explains Jane's fear of losing anyone that was close to her. She was devastated and could only cope with the pain by shutting it out. She was traumatised. Overwhelming childhood experiences like hers can result in states of amnesia to protect the 'inner self'. Jane had mixed feelings about her mother. She oscillated from wanting to be protective towards her to accusing her of driving her father away. What Jane related as her experience of the disappearance of her father after all those years may be a distorted version of the truth. She believed it was the truth. In many instances, recollections are mostly 'explicit'. However, after a traumatic experience like Jane's, seeing her father walk out never to return, can result in trauma. She managed to locate her father's whereabouts when in her twenties. He tried to explain that he was very angry that day and he had to get away. He was unable to confirm that he heard her call out from her window. He was afraid of becoming violent with her mother. Although he thought of her often he could not find the courage to contact her.

10

GROWING UP
EMOTIONALLY:
FROM BIRTH TO ADULTHOOD

This chapter gives a simplified account of human development, beginning from infancy – a crucial stage – followed by childhood, adolescence and adulthood. The various stages of development are considered from a psychoanalytic/psychological perspective, avoiding the jargon as much as possible.

Infancy

Life begins with no choice or certainty as to when, where or how we arrive, who our parents will be, our ethnicity or our creed. The only certainty is that one day we will inevitably die, which we accept without questioning. Initially, we may be as innocent as lambs but develop very differently. Unlike lambs, who are only dependent on being fed by their mother for a brief time, we are totally dependent for a few years and then partially for several more. During those nurturing years, infants are malleable and influenced by the adults immediately around them. Often traditions, culture and socio-economic condition also play a significant role. In some cultures, the mother and infant are left alone to bond and fathers have no role whatsoever in the early nurturing of their offspring.

The process of pregnancy and giving birth is always an anxious time, but the mother/infant scenario is usually one of joy. Prior to the infant's arrival, feelings of expectation, love, joy, fear, doubt, anxiety, trepidation or even negativity may be going through the mother's mind. After the birth, whatever the reactions, they will play a significant role in the relationship between the mother and the infant. The foundations of our emotional development begin from there on. Early good relations go on to cultivate good relationships and vice versa. Psychoanalytic theorists believe that the basis of the individual's personality is moulded during those first few years. During one's daily experiences, we generally react and respond towards others from deep feelings established within us. Continual states of distress during these early years can impact on one's mental equilibrium. Currently, some schools of psychiatry normally based on organic, dysfunctional aspects are now more open to accepting the part of early emotional attachment. Some have traced that patients with severe mental disorders recalled and remembered negative childhood activities, which probably caused their condition.

Until recently, birth was considered as a private activity between mother and midwife, perhaps including a gynaecologist. The mother/infant dyad, especially the religious Christian configuration, has been a popular subject of interest to painters and others. When viewing these paintings, they signify contentment, love and adoration. Unfortunately, reality is often far from what they portray. Experimentally, child psychologists discovered that when the breast milk of one mother on cotton wool was repeatedly placed under the nose of a fairly new born infant belonging to another, it turned its head away. However, if the process was repeated with the infant's mother's milk, the infant made sucking noises. Such sensitivity at such an early age indicates that the infant has a mind of its own. Obviously, the survival instinct is a powerful drive and a very hungry baby will feed from any other source.

The infant is totally dependent on the mother or caregiver for the first few years and to a lesser extent for some years afterwards. Normally, a state of 'reverie' or 'maternal preoccupation', as referred to in psychoanalytic theory, exists between mother and infant. The theme of 'bonding' or close skin contact between the new born and the mother is widely recognised as relevant soon after birth and the early vulnerable stage. Some mothers, for various reasons, are incapacitated to make such contact with their infant, but if a caring other can replace the mother, then babies thrive just as well. The bonding may not be the same, but the intrinsic mechanism of the infant recognises that it is loved. An available mother/caregiver attends to the infant's feelings by instinctively attuning to its need. The baby indicates its feelings physically by smiling, crying, kicking, turning away etc. The mother/caregiver responds to the infant's projection by coming to the rescue and attending to any unpleasant or painful experiences. This kind of processing gives the infant a feeling of security. The infant feels sustained when fed and reacts to the voice, the holding and the sensitivity of the adult. The vulnerable mind has not yet learnt to understand or tolerate anxieties and totally depends on the adult to alleviate distressful or frightening experiences.

During those early years of the convivial mother/infant relationship, the infant feels secure and spurts of self-development occur. Motherhood is a huge responsibility, which influences and determines much of the future of her offspring. The infant's constant demands may make the mother feel inadequate, frustrated or useless. Many mothers cater for the infant's every need for twenty-four hours, seven days a week, for months and years to come. This adds up to very many hours. This is not totally the situation these days as many partners play a vital role in helping with the nurturing of their infants. In an ideal situation, when the mother is aided with some of her responsibilities by her partner or another, she feels emotionally supported. This can make a huge difference to the mother's well-being.

From birth, infants are dominated by some very powerful emotions and they assert these sensitivities most demandingly. Melanie Klein devoted her whole career to the understanding of the infant/mother relationship. She recognised early emotional bonding as unique and without parallel. The infant forcefully makes demands and the mother attunes herself to be constantly available. Immediately after the initial euphoria, the reality of the responsibility sets in when her whole pattern of life changes. She now not only has to think about herself, but also for a very dependent individual. Adjusting to this new lifestyle requires changes that may not always be possible to achieve. Apart from innate qualities, human development is also dependent on learning and babies are great imitators. They have sophisticated sensual mechanisms to cope with good experiences, but many quickly learn to adapt to their environment. It has been noted by infant observers that some babies with depressed mothers are quieter and not as demanding, as discussed below. A happy infant will make pleasant cooing sounds and interact more freely.

Obviously, one inherits various genes from parents, which not only establishes physical features but some emotional characteristics. Under normal circumstances, an infant is born with physical endowment as to whether he or she will be dark or fair and short or tall, as well as their body shape and so forth, but emotional development depends on the parents and caregivers from birth onwards. As adults, one may decide to make appropriate change or adjust through necessity. Unlike the young of animals who become independent from very early on, infants learn as they mature and are dependent on others for this. The immature, vulnerable mind is unable to process or survive without the mother/adult. When the infant or young child feels threatened, its immediate reaction is to cry out for help. If positive nurturing is not readily available, the infant or child feels unsupported. Babies who are often left for long periods without food or attention may become traumatised and it may affect them in some form during their lifetime.

Unnoticed by others, the mother may be depressed. She may be insightful of her infant's need and does her best, but through no deliberate fault on her part her state of mind may have a detrimental effect on the young child. Without intentionally doing deliberate harm to her infant, her emotional state may impact upon it. Consequently, during a later stage, a person having survived under such circumstances may have feelings that are inexplicable to himself and others connected to him. Some act out in certain ways without understanding why they are behaving as they do. Some people have significant and meaningful dreams that link with very early or beginning of life. Perhaps, the need for survival is innately strong and begins from the foetal stage. We are aware that the life instinct is a powerful drive.

The following example may explain how a well-meant decision by a mother very soon after the birth of her infant impacted on her son, years later.

* * *

Sasha, at twenty-six, often felt needy, dependent and emotionally lonely, although he had a loving girlfriend whom in return he loved very much. Even when surrounded by amicable company, he could never be rid of a feeling of loneliness, as if something in his life was missing. He had a good, well-paid job and understanding colleagues, whom he often socialised with. His girlfriend, although very caring, complained that he was too clingy. He decided to come for psychotherapy 'to sort himself out'. Not long after he started he casually mentioned that he had a recurring dream. It was so stupid that it became a joke between him and his girlfriend. At times when he was pre-occupied she would laughingly say, 'Thinking about your friend who missed the bus!' After some hesitancy he related, "I am usually running for a bus and am aware that someone is right behind me also trying to catch it. I manage to get on, but the other couldn't make it. I stretch my hand out to help him, but he is unable to grab my hand. I am upset as I see him standing there as the bus moves away and his image stays with me as I wake up."

The dream left him puzzled and disturbed him. Now that it had recurred intermittently he thought that it must be of some significance. He had had the same dream that morning. He revealed that whenever he had the dream he felt preoccupied and was unable to function at work as usual. This annoyed him because it ruined his day. He also experienced feelings of insecurity and became over-worried if his girlfriend was late from work. This started rows between them. She said he was being over-anxious and too clingy.

After much deliberation on the subject, he volunteered something his aunt had once said. He had been rushing out at the time and was not paying much attention to her. She usually talked too much. Whatever it was did not register at the time, except that he remembered her saying to his mother, something about 'wondering what the twin would have been like'. Through our discussion during that session, he decided to ask his aunt if she had said anything about a twin. His aunt refused to talk about it and said that he was imagining things. He then brought up the subject in the presence of his mother and father, on a Sunday when his aunt usually came for lunch. His mother looked shocked and accused her sister of stirring up the past. His father looked up from reading the Sunday papers and said to his mother, "It is time we told him. It cannot do him any harm. He is old enough to understand."

It was then clarified that his identical twin had died at birth. His parents believed there was no reason to tell him. Why trouble him unnecessarily? He had been healthy and well. What difference would it make to him now? They were pleased he had survived. Watching him grow up as a healthy baby had diluted his mother's experience of loss. Then, the subject seemed to have disappeared from their minds until he brought it up. Sasha felt disturbed about hearing this. The dream now made sense. He was alive, but his brother had died. Trying to help the person catch the bus now made some sense to him. He would have been very close to his twin during the foetal stage.

This explained him being clingy to his girlfriend – someone nearest and dearest to him. During therapy, gaining access to the emotional functioning of an individual often leads to remembering dreams. The method often induces the past emotional life to come to the forefront in this manner.

Infant Observation Studies

Psychoanalytic observation studies concentrate on the mother/caregiver – infant relationship. Close scrutiny of the dyad had shown some very remarkable interactions, wherein the infant had displayed some intense feelings. Central to my discussion is that emotional development for a well-balanced life depends on the inner state or personality beginning from those formative years. As previously conveyed, much of our early nurturing plays a significant role in influencing the rest of our emotional lifetime. The Psychoanalytic Observation Study of an Infant was originally introduced by Esther Bick (5) as an important pre-requisite for the training of child psychotherapists. The trainee undertakes to observe a mother and her infant from soon after the birth of the baby until it is two years old on a weekly basis at the same time and day. Bick felt that this kind of experiential knowledge was essential to understand the non-verbal communication of an infant or very young child. An infant who is hungry or afraid cannot verbalise those feelings. It panics and cries. Alternately, an infant who is content and happy coos and smiles. The vulnerable developing mind during those formative years require intense understanding and tolerance. Although they are strong willed, they are also totally dependent on the adult and therefore can be easily influenced. Continual unwarranted neglect can lead to psychopathological states at a later stage.

During infant observation studies, as many of the activities as possible between the dyad are scrutinised. This includes the infant's reactions and behavioural responses to the mother's presence, as well as when she is not with the infant. Attachment, separation and loss provoke anxiety and anger, as suggested by John Bowlby (7), who explained, 'Psychoanalysts and ethnologists are agreed that a principal key to the understanding of any sort of behaviour is to study it developmentally. Nowhere is this perspective more necessary than in the study of fear behaviour in man.' He goes on to qualify that this starts during infancy when the infant is separated from its source of survival.

Behaviour is the outer manifestation of inner feeling. Many adult training institutions have included the methodology as a necessity to qualify. Listening and observing the patient both play a significant role during an analytic session. Often, patients withdraw or oscillate from infantile states of mind to that of the adult. Observational studies have also influenced other areas of work to gain insight into the emotional life of people of all ages who are unable to verbalise their feelings and thoughts. Students undertake to observe young nursery age children, people suffering from dementia and institutionalised old people. Professionals and clinicians undertake to attend some training courses to learn how to improve their observational skills. As Rustin (6) explains, 'The methods of psychoanalytic infant observation… explain their relationship on the one hand to more behavioural and explicitly 'scientific' modes of study of infancy and, on the other, to psychoanalytic clinical practice.'

When working with an adult, concentration on any cues, linked to inner states of the mind related to infancy and young childhood days may give the therapist an idea of what might be causing the current distress or unsociable behaviour. Psychoanalytic theory, from Freud's legacy, as earlier mentioned, significantly explains that every sensitivity and experience from birth is stored in the mind as 'unconscious processes'. To begin with, the infant is influenced by the mother/caregiver, then the father and various other parties that one is surrounded with from birth.

Child development researchers studied the effects of mirroring in infant behaviour. They asked mothers of young babies to make certain facial expressions conveying different emotions, gestures and sounds while holding their infants in front of them. The babies responded by imitating these expressions. If the expressions were distressing, the babies found them unbearable and cried or turned away. Good nurturing involves being attuned intrinsically, in order to alleviate the infant's anxieties. But if the mother/caregiver is unable to provide this and the infant continually experiences stressful situations, the infant's emotionality is affected, which, in turn, disrupts its functioning. Psychologists discuss these experiences as 'object relations'. Failure to have a good object during mothering impacts on the infant in various ways and the impact may affect the rest of the infant's lifetime.

There are numerous and varied types of mother/infant relationships, from loving, understanding and positively well-established ones to those that entail deprivation, cruelty and insecurity. My purpose is not to understand or write about the negative aspects of child rearing, but to draw attention to how our later behaviour is associated and affected with these earlier feelings. During my experience of working with very young, vulnerable children in the NHS at child care and mental health clinics, I noted the consequences of poor mothering and how this impacted on some of the children. This is not a criticism of the mother, just an observation, because, as aforementioned, some mothers are in a vulnerable state and require emotional support to help with a demanding infant.

However, many overcome the negative experiences of early days and make improvements for the better. Education providers now recognise that mental problems are prevalent amongst young children and adolescents. As a result, schools now appoint therapists or counsellors to support children with emotional problems. This enables them to adjust and develop a stronger personality leading to successful lifestyles. It is common knowledge that some adults who experienced the most atrocious and painful childhood experiences learn to integrate their negative experiences and become healthy, successful people. Historically, it is not uncommon to read about such individuals who have become influential adults in many fields. Some have bequeathed us with legacies of their knowledge and creativity.

Observation studies from birth to the age of two have produced some interesting behavioural patterns linked to emotionality. The following vignettes from two observations explain some very simple activities of these infants. The responses and reactions of their respective mothers were also noted. The examples deliberately represent mothers and infants of the same age, ethnicity and from a similar socio-economic background. Both mothers had given up their respective jobs to be with their first babies and had looked forward to starting a family. Both obviously loved their infants. The second mother was suffering from a mild form of postnatal depression from after the birth. As the observations progressed her mental health improved and by the time her son was eighteen months old she was not taking the medication.

a) Observation of a containing mother/infant relationship:

I was with a mother and her four-month-old infant, Sean. He was lying on a padded mat, which had an overhead structure of colourful mobiles of various shapes. Sean could touch and safely pull some of these down. Some would spring back, and I observed his delightful smile whenever this happened. The mother responded to his happy sounds. At one point, Sean's mother abruptly stood up and, without saying a word, walked out to the kitchen to make a cup of tea. The infant immediately stopped playing, turned, glanced at the doorway and started to make moaning noises. He started kicking agitatedly. The mother called out, "What's all that about? I'll be back very soon. You should know that!" She started humming a little tune.

The infant stopped kicking, turned his head towards the kitchen door and the moaning stopped. As soon as his mother returned with the tea, his expression altered to delight and he gave her a beaming smile. She rewarded him by picking him up, hugging and showering him with kisses. When she placed him on the mat again, he gazed rapturously at her before resuming his play. Throughout my time with

Sean and his mother, I noticed that she intermittently turned towards him and appraised his efforts.

This mother was in touch with her infant's feelings. He, in turn, experienced the security he needed when he felt anxious about being abandoned. He probably did not understand the actual words, but the caring tone and immediate response assured him that she was there for him. Soon after Sean's second birthday, the couple were contemplating having a second child and Sean was taken to nursery two mornings a week. He was upset and cried when his mother left. He became anxious, which is a normal reaction of separation anxieties. Once he understood and felt assured that his mother would return to take him home, he relaxed. The early experiences of containment of his anxieties helped him to adjust to his first major separation and loss. During the weeks before he was due to go to play school, his mother frequently spoke to him about it. He had visited with her and to some extent was prepared for this new adventure. Initially he clung to her and refused to let her go. Eventually through persuasion he went with his care worker, following her around and wanted her approval of what he did. After the first few days, assured that his mother would return to take him home, his inner feeling of security grew. This enabled him to feel confident and he became adventurous and explored the wider environment of the play school. After a few weeks he looked forward to and enjoyed his time at the nursery.

b) Observation of the uncontained infant situation:

The second infant, Roy, was also four months old and was lying in his carrycot. There was an overhead, semi-circular structure with various soft toys, including a cat and a book, attached to the cot. The infant quietly observed them. He tentatively touched the cat. The family had a cat as a pet. He was not unhappy but was expressionless. He occasionally kicked and threw his hands about, then sucked his thumb.

Then, he started to pout and began to cry loudly. His mother looked at him but did nothing. His crying grew louder. The mother without looking at him, said, "What is it now, Roy?" After a few minutes she walked up to him. "You can't be wet. It is not yet time for your feed." She never smiled or touched him while she stuck a dummy into his mouth. He sucked fervently, remained quiet for a few minutes and then turned his head with a painful expression. The dummy fell out of his mouth and he immediately started crying loudly. She picked him up and, holding him upright against her shoulder, she patted him on the back. I could see his face and notice he had shut his eyes. He quietened down. The mother turned around, looked at me and said, "I don't know what's bothering him. He was changed and fed only a little while ago, just before you arrived."

I was there in the role of an observer and not to share my feelings or make any personal comments. To acknowledge her remark, and not make her feel I was unfriendly, I said, "He has quietened down."

She continued to pat him in a distracted way. She talked about the weekend, when she was expecting her parents. She was very much looking forward to that as her mother would help with the night feed. Roy, at this stage, was being bottle fed. Her husband often took over at weekends, but he was also tired and needed a rest. She added that she was on medication and it was not advisable to feed Roy. She often spoke about his feeding and of him being a very hungry baby. With a smile she added, "I don't know where all the food is going to. He is not overweight and never seems satisfied." It was not my role to get into any discussion about her problems. I never learnt when her depression started or what medication she was on. Physically, Roy was a healthy baby, but he was not a happy one. I felt sorry for the mother. She seemed desperately in need of mothering. I could tell that she was pleased to have me visit. I wondered about her own childhood.

Even though she had come off the antidepressants by the time Roy was a year old she still had difficulties with him. The lack of early reverie between mother and infant was noticeable. She automatically tended to his needs. However, she lacked the capacity to show any tangible delight or loving adoration towards Roy. Materially, he lacked nothing, but emotionally he seemed deprived of that special loving closeness that is expected between mother and infant during the first few months. Roy often played very quietly, as if he did not want to upset his mother. At times, I thought he looked sad and remote. He was a well-behaved, good little boy as if aware of his mother's delicate health.

Discussion:

The differences between Sean and Roy were very noticeable. Sean was full of energy, active, creative and adventurous as expected of a young child of his age. He smiled, made friends with other children and grown-ups after the initial and normal reservation. By two he had quite a range of vocabulary and started speaking in phrases, also imitating a few short sentences. Roy on the other hand was insular, preferred to play on his own, hardly smiled and was not very adventurous. He lacked confidence, clung to his mother and hardly spoke. He was bright and understood most things addressed to him. What they would be like when they became adults I would never know. But my understanding is that young children from very early on adapt to and respond to the mother's interaction. Secure feelings during early nurturing play a significant role in the future development of the personality. This does not mean that Sean will be a great success or Roy a failure. But, I think it will make a difference to how they cope with life experiences and relate to others, during adolescence, adulthood and later life.

Authorities on infant observation have noted that reassurance during the early months provides stability. An infant with this kind of secure base copes more positively whenever any form of anxiety sets in. Unlike young animals, the human infant is still unable to seek the mother when it is hungry and is totally dependent on the adult for nourishment. Should the feed be continually delayed and not come as expected, anxieties and terrors multiply and the infant feels it is going to die. Although they feel incapacitated, the innate, strong survival instincts encourage them to demand until they get the feed. In normal circumstances, they get what they want. Life and death instincts are predominant in the infant. From about the age of six months, although no longer a symbiotic relationship, the mother is intuitively in touch with her young infant. The failure of the mother/caregiver to lessen the infant's or her own anxieties may result in frustration, leaving the infant feeling afraid, vulnerable and insecure.

At about six months, the infant's explorative senses make him become aware of a third person, namely the father or another, and then others. Then, the infant starts to crawl and becomes more aware of the surroundings. He propels himself to become physically explorative and adventurous – the precursor to independence. His senses become more prominent and he is daring enough to become adventurous. However, he is unable to differentiate between safety and danger, but he does sense fear. If he feels afraid, he will cling to his mother or the caring adult. As he develops, he asserts his independence when the tantrums begin. This is widely accepted as a normal phase of emotional growth, but the toddler also needs to learn to differentiate between safe and harmful activities. He acquires language skills and other physical functioning aspects.

During infancy and early childhood, the individual experiences periods of psychic gains as well as losses. The ability to process the losses originates from internal feelings of containment acquired during the nurturing stage. Every experience, whether positive or negative, will remain with him for the rest of his lifetime. As explained earlier, from time to time, many forgotten experiences from childhood are suddenly recalled. They can either be pleasurable or disturbing. Frequently, some present activity or communication triggers off an old, long-forgotten image from memory. Everything we touch, smell, hear and see stays in the human mind, as earlier noted. Our daily life swivels around the process of communication, which matters to us in the way that food, water, air and other bodily functions are necessary for good physical health – as Wilfred Bion conveyed.

However, there are the healthy aspects of nurturing that stir up some negative, painful feelings and anxieties of separation. For example, when a child first experiences the separation from a familiar environment and goes to play school. These days for various reasons, many infants separate from their mothers much earlier and the rearing is taken over by others. Regardless, a very young child with an emotionally secure base will cope as well. Although he may feel uncertain of the new environment, he is more inclined to adjust and settle down as he trusts the adults around him. With a good basic internal structure, these separations, although anxiety-provoking, are positive steps towards psychic growth. Independence and a positive frame of mind to overcome such separations cultivate a mature, independent personality. Positive, good nurturing during the first few years are essential.

Childhood

For centuries, young children had been regarded as miniature adults. They were dressed similarly but not allowed to voice their feelings or thoughts as individuals. The twentieth century transformed our perception when child developmental psychologists and child psychotherapists began to coherently and constructively study them as individuals who had their own feelings and thoughts. From there on, the infant and young child were perceived differently. They were respected as having individualistic mental and emotional processes although they were dependent on the adult for care and nourishment. Childhood, although a very vulnerable and dependent period, is an exciting and explorative time. The young child indicates experiences by the quality of urgency in which he expresses his personal feelings. The more urgent the need, the more demanding they become. It is an exciting time for both the child and parents, as new experiences are developmentally displayed. Nevertheless, children need to be carefully watched and monitored. They attempt to physically and intellectually mature, become more and more explorative, and continually try to display new skills, without the hindsight of danger. Before the acquisition of language, young children focus on action they have perceived, and which they imitate from memory and foresight. They purposefully develop practical skills.

Young children have striking responses to music long before the acquisition of verbal skills. Without prompting they make physical movements and keep time to music. During this period, their singular words, such as 'Dada', 'Mama', 'me-me', 'ta-ta' and 'bye-bye', sound like musical notes. Although most of the nursery rhymes have horrific endings it is the music and not the words they are attuned to. From this early stage, a multidimensional and garbled form of language is used for communication. This develops into using phrases and simple sentences. Following this, they acquire language. Mimicking and imitating expressions they hear, although beyond their comprehension, are often used. The stories that are read to them are reiterated word for word from memory, and at times, flow from one to another into a lengthy monologue. This phase is one in which their curiosity is aroused. The child progresses to asking questions, commonly recognised as the 'why phase', leading to how, when, where and what, often to the exasperation of the adult.

As non-discerning individuals, eager to experiment and try new adventures, young children require sustained care. They are still mentally and physically fragile. Often, their curiosity overrides danger, as they do not seem to have any real sense of it. It is necessary to continuously watch, help and support them, so that they cope during times of vulnerability and insecurity. This kind of positive nurturing, while respecting the need for independence, helps children to experience good object relations and to develop a stable state of mind. Most young children cultivate a sense of independence as they venture into the world of the nursery after the initial anxieties of separation. Noticeably, they seem to adopt a dual personality. They are independent and obedient at nursery, but they play up and regress to a state of being a baby at home. This phase can continue for some time and, in some cases, is still evident in adults. This depends on the extent of the collusive aspect between the individual and the mother/other.

From personal experience and observation of very young children, I have noted two categories of mental functioning. The first swivels around a personal, idiosyncratic, unfathomable phantasy world, which is often not communicated to those around. The child does not seem to be consciously thinking about what he is doing. He is uninhibited and honest and seems to be inspired from within. When questioned, the child is unable to give a clear reason for what he is doing. On a parallel with this kind of functioning, there is the conscious, practical, reasonable and logical part of himself, he shares through the medium of language. As the child develops physically his mental processes also progress to a higher level. He combines his feelings and thoughts in explicit language, enabling him to communicate with others.

For example: I was with a three-year-old, joining in some of his play. He picked up a box containing his railway set and placed it on the floor near me. Puzzled, I watched him as he placed some of the tracks all over the room. He then emptied the rest of the contents in the middle of the floor, mumbling to himself. He looked keenly at the pile, then collected the scattered pieces and placed them on top of the others. When I asked him what he was doing, he ignored me, not even bothering to look at me. I wondered if he had heard me or whether he was too involved in his internal world, oblivious of anyone else. Then, he replaced all the pieces into the box and pushed it aside. He looked preoccupied.

Soon after, he smiled and carefully chose certain pieces. As he was doing this, he looked directly at me and explained, "I am going to build a track with a station and a bridge. I need the tracks, the station, the fat controller and the trains." He named each piece as he took it out of the box and then announced, "I am the station master."

He continued to communicate what he was doing as he meticulously connected some of the track to the station and went on to build the bridge but was unable to do so because it had no supports to hold it up. He looked around and I reminded him that he had not taken out the supports. He looked at me critically and said, "I forgot the pylons." He proceeded to look for them in his box, found them and with a big smile announced, "Here they are!"

When he had completed his task, he looked at me proudly and said, "You can have Emily now and I will have Thomas."

What was going on in his mind during the first part of his activity, I could not imagine? He was obviously engrossed with his inner world. But a part of him was in touch with the external surroundings as he loudly explained what he was going to do. Fascinated, intrigued and impressed, I watched him realising that he had not only registered what I had said and was quick to correct me. During my previous visit, he had taken me to his room to proudly show me a huge track layout he had done with his father. It was obvious that words like 'station master' and 'pylon' had been used then, which he had remembered and recalled. Perhaps he wanted to impress me with his acquisition of words or perhaps he was just enjoying his play and proud that he could explain it to me.

On another occasion when I was playing with him, he stopped what he was doing, looked at me seriously and unexpectedly exclaimed, "I have so many things to do before I die."

I was shocked and could not immediately respond. I recalled that their cat had recently been put to sleep. He was very upset and was told briefly by his parents about dying. I said that he did have a lot to do, such as going to nursery, big school, college and then work like his daddy etc. To my relief, he moved on to playing and talking about other things. I would never know what was on his mind when he made that remark. Was he conveying something through his feelings of the experience he recently had or was this an intellectual activity coming from some associated thoughts? It is common knowledge that imitating adults plays a significant role during those early years.

A happy and contented childhood period is crucial for coping with all kinds of situations for the rest of one's life. Childhood is also a time for integration as the thinking process develops. During normal circumstances, this is a carefree and enjoyable period of one's life. Unavoidably, growing up also entails painful and unpleasant emotional and physical experiences, but with loving support, the young child learns to cope with these negative experiences, which become the foundation for dealing with future hazards during adulthood. Happy childhood memories linger on, but disastrous encounters can compel a child to become defensive and repress such feelings for self-protection. All experiences are internalised and effect one's future life.

Separation from the mother/caregiver and the home environment begins at a much earlier stage these days. Several adults may play a role during those important early years. Through financial circumstances, many grandparents help to rear and play a significant part in a young child's life. If a parent is in a vulnerable mental state, the shared responsibility may be to the child's advantage. Nurseries differ, but basically, good caring involves understanding and encouragement to cultivate good social habits. Under normal circumstances, the parents and other adults fulfil the need of the young child, recognising that some things are beyond his capability. Patience, tolerance and understanding of their communication shape the young child's future. The importance of healthy emotional development during those early formative years is broadly understood as the basis for mental well-being for years to come. If the foundation during those formative years feels secure, then it is the grounding for stability. The individual feels better equipped to cope with adverse situations in the future. Unfortunately, not every child is reared in an ideal home situation or nursery, as we so often read about in books or as portrayed on television and in films.

The educational system also plays a significant role in moulding a child's early years. Children often trust adults to take care of them. Unfortunately, this is now considered as 'false belief'. Daily, one notes that vulnerable young people have been most offensively and despicably treated, physically or sexually abused. This has resulted in all kinds of mental disorders for many at various stages during their lives. Other punitive treatments of the past, like caning, to morally reform young people, have caused distress and have proved to be detrimental to their emotional functioning. Some of these past negative experiences have been unwittingly or deliberately expressed through the medium. Equivocally, any experience that is ignored for whatever reason – whether associated with pain or shame, or if it is beyond comprehension – remains as a shadow in the unconscious. There is no denying that the impact of feelings and the major part they play during our daily lives, whether we wish to believe it or not, happens.

Adolescence

Adolescence is probably the most fraught stage of human development. It is a time when one is no longer a child, nor yet matured to adulthood. Potential physical growth coinciding with emotional development cause unexpected disturbances to many an adolescent. The movement towards independence becomes more and more desirable. Simultaneously, this is also perceived with some trepidation as feelings of being between and betwixt become confusing. Contradictory inner turbulences persist, while the pressure to grow up interchanges with the desire to stay with childhood feelings and characteristics, for fear of moving into unknown territories. These inner struggles and conflicts may make the adolescent feel insecure, as the pressure to move away from dependency to independence grows. Inevitable physical, adult sensations may feel pleasurable and desirable but also confusing. It is a stage that is often intellectually understood by the adolescent but unpredictable until personally experienced.

To feel emotionally secure, many adolescents become part of a group as 'group culture' gives a sense of security. Characteristics of inferiority may be disowned and projected onto another. Pseudo confidence may be gained by being in identification with another, giving a false sense of security. With some, the intensity of being involved with dangerous activities feel desirable. Secrecy from parents and others in authority is common during this stage of development. Disowning troublesome feelings onto a weaker member of the group may bring a sense of relief, however short-lived. Rivalry for leadership by stronger members of the group causes problems when splitting may occur within the group. A powerful or self-willed individual may persistently dominate, undermining his rivals. The weaker members may be too afraid to protest for fear of being ostracised. The adolescent's pseudo maturity may, at times, collapse and he may be persuaded to make a fool of himself or become the target of his peers. Adolescents can be very cruel if they suspect weakness in another. Bullying is common during this stage, when one's weakness may be projected as that of another. Under their 'false front', bullies are usually found to be despicable, shallow characters who are hiding their inferiority complexes. Failure to cope could lead one astray, with such unsavoury activities as drug taking or alcoholism.

This is also the phase of the lifespan when one is anxious to become independent. Contradictorily he may be reluctant to take on the new responsibilities that go with growing up. As the adolescent tries to move away from parental control, his confusion and unpredictable state of mind may simultaneously make him more dependent on adults. But later adolescence is also a period when a new awareness of personal status and changes becomes unavoidable. Major physical changes and feelings may feel threatening, bewildering or incapacitating, leaving the adolescent feeling as though they are in a state of uncertainty or despair. Separation from parents at this stage is very different from that of early childhood. The young child eventually understands that he will be returning home to his familiar surroundings and be back with the parents. Older adolescents do come home over the holidays, but this is generally more of a temporary nature. Living away from home in an environment surrounded by people of a similar age and having to entirely fend for oneself may bring on certain anxieties. Decision making without the help and support of parents or family members may be bewildering. The new level of responsibility may lead to confusion and distress. Commitments, like paying bills and preparing meals, become a daily reality. With the loss of childhood and the earlier stage of adolescence, the latter stage brings on new personal experiences, as impulses increase an inner sense of reflection. Challenges of a different nature confront and preoccupy the later stage of adolescence as he moves on to becoming a young adult.

From this stage, the movement towards adulthood through newfound sexual desires and aggressive connected feelings alter mental functioning. New experiences in relation to the opposite gender may create states of excitement, as well as conflict, anger and disappointment. During this later adolescent stage, an inherent sense of sexual identity often leads to a sustainable and intimate relationship with a partner. Other responsibilities such as thinking about new placements, new institutions, authorities, society and one's parents from a different, adult perspective evoke other feelings of responsibility. It is also an unpredictable stage when adolescents may move forward developmentally and then suddenly, for some unknown reason, are unable to make the expected progress. Doubtless, this can be a feature at any stage of the lifespan. A common feature of life is, while detaching from one state of being, one becomes attached to other structures.

Inappropriate behaviour, perhaps allowed at home, may not be approved of or considered kindly elsewhere. Societal demands combined with achieving educationally or performing adequately at work necessitates tolerance and patience. Not surprisingly, adolescents fall into disrepute or give into feelings of anger and become destructive. Vandalism is the outer consequence, carried out in a brainless manner, as a way of venting inner disturbances. It is not surprising that adolescence is considered as the most difficult phase of one's life. One is not a child any longer, yet one is not an adult. Which phase do you adopt to behave normally?

Other factors, such as the genes one inherits, helpful or discouraging parental pressure also play a significant role during adolescence. Although siblings share the same biological parents, the same environment and often similar experiences during those early formative years, they may vastly differ and drift in very different directions during adolescence. One hopes that an earlier secure base will come to the rescue and positively influence times of difficulties. Some things may be doubted at first and may feel confusing, challenging and intellectually debated or they are generally accepted as sensible. Emotional growing up entails trial and error, as one learns from one's mistakes. Older adolescents gradually find their own goals and act according to their unique and individualistic personalities. Unfortunately, for some known or unknown reason, an individual may be influenced to go off at a tangent contrary to his usual self. Unexpected and unforeseen demands may have proved difficult to cope with and a failure to make the necessary adjustments required. One may overcome this phase, through being rescued by the earlier secure grounding and attain an inner state of tranquillity. Some may require professional support to overcome this state of mind as the following excerpt indicates.

* * *

I was contacted to see an older adolescent who was doing a post graduate degree, which was going very well until he suddenly became depressed, lost interest in his work and spent many hours listlessly on his own. None of his colleagues or tutors could understand the sudden change in him. His personal tutor became quite concerned and persuaded him to contact me. I discovered that he had thought his parents' relationship was fine until they suddenly announced they were separating. Not long after, to add to the shock, he was told that his mother had been diagnosed with cancer, which was fortunately treatable. Simultaneously, he found out that his father had moved in with another woman that he had been seeing for some time. The shock was too much to bear. He hated his father and blamed him for being the cause of his mother's illness. He refused to have anything to do with him, deciding to forfeit continuing at college because his father was paying his fees. He also decided to take care of his mother until his older sister, who lived abroad, could make the appropriate arrangements to come.

After several meetings, he confessed that his mother had told him that she had made the decision to separate from his father. They had lived separate lives for some time now. His relationship with the other woman started long after his mother had refused to be with his father. He realised it was unfair to blame his father and it was unnecessary for him to have given up college. His father was doing his best and cared about his welfare. His mother also tried to explain that she was still on friendly terms with his father and he was not to be blamed.

It took some time for the young man to register that his parents had amicably decided to separate. The break-up of the marriage was not his father's fault. The shock of realising that his parents had separated blocked out the truth. His own disturbing feelings towards his mother also played some part in his anger towards his father. His mother had always come over as vulnerable and delicate, and he had felt very protective towards her. Fortunately, he went back to his studies and, while still in therapy, successfully completed his degree. Eventually, he not only understood the reality of what had happened, but also his own state of mind. By the end of his therapy, he was dating a girl whom he seemed very fond of. Nevertheless, it took some time before he had a reasonable and friendly relationship with his father again.

Some thoughts

In cases like the above, support from parents or other adults, although readily available or adequate, may not be enough. The adolescent has his own internal strife that may become confused with the outer reality. The home environment may influence the adolescent who is perhaps struggling with his own new experiences of chronological and emotional maturation. Adding to this, the above adolescent had to come to terms with new changes in the outer home situation. This created further turmoil and conflicts. The required external organisation and adjustments were beyond the adolescent's capabilities. This young man's father had to often be away from home and he psychically took on the role of being his mother's protector. His older brother lived many miles away and had a young family of his own. My patient became very attached to his sickly mother and blamed his father. He believed that his father was the perpetrator who ended the marriage, resulting in her becoming ill. Therefore, he could not accept that his father was paying for his course fees.

Adulthood

At birth, our parents or caregivers may phantasise a future for us. During our younger days, we, ourselves have aspirations and goals we wish to achieve. Young people's dreams of love and the instinctive desire to procreate play a significant role with many. Some people achieve their aims and lead satisfactory lifestyles, but how many adults can really say that they are totally content as they have achieved everything they desired and that they could wish for nothing more. As discussed earlier, whatever we do during our lifetime depends on some of our early nurturing. However, one can never be in total control. Unavoidable, outer circumstances and disasters may have the opposite effect and impact in a negative way. Appropriate decisions can only be made if we confront our feelings, honestly, and process them by differentiating and separating any wishful thinking and phantasy from reality. This is necessary before we make any further appropriate decision. It is only then that one can maintain a well-balanced inner or psychic state. Painful experiences in their raw state may not always be easy to confront if the pain is unbearable. Sooner or later, such experiences need processing before a state of well-being may be achieved. We come with some legacy from our childhood days, both positive and negative that remain as part of our 'inner world'. The question arises as to how we cope with negative, early experiences that are evoked during our adult lifetime. If clearly thought out, we can more often make appropriate decisions. Mental pain may be experienced before some decisive result can be achieved. As mentioned in Section One, we cannot be rid of past experiences, but we can accept and integrate them as part of our personality.

Adulthood is normally the longest period of our lifetime and is usually filled with an immense amount of varied activities. The everyday, busy lifestyles of most adults involve studying, working, nurturing and other responsibilities. Many may not have time for contemplation and reflection on one's negative actions. Momentarily, some nagging feelings of doubt may occur, leaving one feeling uncomfortable, but they are soon forgotten. During other times of recalling such incidents, one may be distracted by some of the many demanding commitments. More serious negative or even harmful reactions may be explained away as necessary or beyond control. In the twenty-first century, for many, the competitive drive for power establishes a place in society. Women can choose whether they want to have a child or not, which has led some to forfeit motherhood. Many are content with the lifestyle they have chosen. Others have retained their feminine role together with their career status to become successful in both areas.

Modernism has significantly altered the female and male roles. Some men now opt to nurture their young, while their partners continue to be the provider. The demands of the cost of living often influence the state of affairs. In most cases, if the female partner earns more, it seems appropriate for the father to do the nurturing. Also, there may be fathers who make better carers than the mothers and choose to nurture their young. Whoever takes on the day-to-day care, the adults are responsible for the psychological development of the young. A mother who has experienced difficulties with her own mother may feel inadequate or afraid of doing to her child what she has undergone. A father who felt deprived of his infancy and childhood may feel an urge to give his child what he missed out on. Alternatively, a parent may persuade a child to behave the way he or she experienced during an earlier stage to re-experience what their experience had been. This may be either beneficial or harmful to the offspring. Manifold, psychic convolutions for why we behave the way we do make up our personality. Nevertheless, adulthood is a time of responsibility for one's actions as well as being supportive for dependents. The old expression of 'the nuclear family' is now somewhat outdated, but it has not disappeared altogether. Many single parents nurture and bring up emotionally healthy families. However, during life's journey, one may be side tracked and it is not often easy to go back and trace the right path. One may have to reconsider and accept the pitfalls so that reconciliation can take place.

There is no idealised version of existence under which we live or a perfect blueprint to direct us, especially during the changing conditions and demands made in the current climate. All one can do is be honest with oneself and deliver to one's ability. This may not always be simple or straightforward. Current cultural changes and loss of traditions with a fast-developing emphasis on intergenerational associations require mental adjustments. Transmigration, a common feature of the twenty-first century requires emotional adjustments and learning of new skills. Adulthood is also a time for continual learning to keep pace with new electronic technology. To maintain a state of psychic equilibrium one has to be honest with oneself. Many adults try to adjust totally from an intellectual stance and are continually in a state of internal debate or turmoil. It may help them to attain some peace of mind if they give themselves some space to try and process and evaluate the true situation. Through paying attention to their true feelings to acquire individuality, rather than follow the norm.

Parents may realise that they are not in the same frame of mind as one of their adult offspring. Paradoxically, the latter may not be able to recognise some of the pitfalls of their activity or idea. Does the adult then kill their initiative and enthusiasm by warning the young person or let him learn through his mistakes? Obviously, if the action involves danger, the adult would explain this to the young person. Adulthood is therefore a time of immense, unfathomable responsibilities. It is not only a time of thinking about oneself, but others in many different situations. For example, being a parent or in charge of subordinates at a workplace, or as an educationalist moulding young lives. Adults are often in very powerful positions without realising their status.

However, there are others who find that they cannot cope with the mental and emotional strain and it leads them to despair, anxiety, depression or even a mental breakdown. Human behaviour is a complex process and what might have seemed 'the right thing to do' at the time or something done spontaneously may result in feelings of guilt, being a burden or hopelessness. During times of danger, strong, instinctive, involuntary reactions may arise to ward off the threat or danger. The inner need for self-protection and survival is innately strong. With hindsight some behaviour that may have felt pleasurable or positive at the time may be felt to be far from the truth, leaving one feeling guilty or remorseful. Inevitably, it is too late to change or undo what has been done. Some activities from our earlier days remain in stasis for long periods of time, but they may suddenly be triggered off and influence our adult life at a later stage as explained in Section One.

With the passing of time, those guilt-ridden feelings become shelved somewhere as grey areas of one's life experiences. To confide in another, no matter how trusting that person may be, becomes more and more difficult. These shelved feelings may seem less relevant, be totally forgotten and yet remain with us as irrepressible secrets stored in what we know as the mind. In some people, as discussed earlier, trauma may make them wipe out the incident entirely. More often, though, identification with a current topic or event opens the floodgates and the experience is recalled or remembered. Occasionally, an unexpected silent, persistent inner voice suddenly demands acknowledgement. Jealousy and envious feelings are also characteristics that may prove troublesome to one's inner state. Obviously, good memories also get triggered off, are readily accepted and once more indirectly enjoyed. Adulthood is still a time for growth, not only in the acquisition of new skills and the learning of new activities, but also in the emotional state. Adulthood personifies some intriguing characteristics rooted in the inner world

Human behaviour is unpredictable as it involves characteristics like love, hate, anger, gratitude, ambition, rivalry, jealousy, envy, greed, lust and other emotional and behavioural unconscious states of mind. These are unexpectedly triggered off and displayed in the conscious world. Shakespeare significantly pointed out that:

All the world's a stage,
And all the men and women merely players,
They have their exits and their entrances,
And one man in his time plays many parts,
His acts being seven ages.

As You Like It: Act 2, Scene 7

Later life

Following a long period of caring and doing for others, life inevitably moves on to one becoming an older adult, followed by later life and old age, when dramatic changes take place. During this stage of adulthood, very different thoughts and feelings begin to preoccupy and influence an individual. Children and their families transmigrate or geographically move long distances away. Spouses may have left or have died. Degenerative physical and or mental experiences are not uncommon. This time of adulthood requires several kinds of adjustments. Baby boomers expect and require more as their right in comparison to their ancestors. They not only persistently demand but more often achieve their goals. Facilities for many older adults to continue to learn and productively deliver in various forms, intellectually, physically or both, are now more available through the colleges of the Third Age. These facilities give many an older adult much enjoyment, companionship and a purpose in life.

Others go back to being employed on a part-time basis, giving them the extra financial support they so much need, while some continue to work long after retirement. Sadly, and unfortunately, many need care and support for mental and physical disabilities. On an optimistic level, this is often also a time for re-figuration, readjustment and contemplation of the future, which may be a long and propitious one or the beginning of a disastrous ageing process. Aspirations and ambition may not have come to fruition, making it a time for reassessment and acceptance of failures. The relevant fact is to be positive and bear in mind what Longfellow suggested.

> *Morituri salutamus*
> *It is too late! Ah nothing is too late*
> *Till the tired heart shall cease to palpitate,*
> *Cato learned Greek at eighty, Sophocles*
> *Wrote his grand Oedipus and Simonides*
> *Bore off the prize of verse from his comperes*
> *When each had numbered more than four score years*
> *Chaucer at Woodstock with the nightingales*
> *At sixty wrote the Canterbury Tales;*
> *Goethe at Weimer, toiling to the last,*
> *Completed Faust when eighty years were past,*
> *These are indeed exceptions, but they show*
> *How far the gulf stream of our youth may flow*
> *Into the arctic regions of our lives…*
> *For age is opportunity no less*
> *Than youth itself, though in another dress*
> *And as the evening twilight fades away*
> *The sky is filled with stars, invisible by day.*

11

THE TALKING CURE

The beginning

Historically, the study and concentration on understanding feelings and the impact they have on our daily lives first came to light during the late nineteenth century. A group of medical professionals in Vienna, specialising in neurological illnesses and working with institutionalised patients suffering mental problems, decided to reconsider and find other methods of treatment. The norm was to concentrate on chemical-physical and pathological facts, particularly connected with the brain. Apart from medication some very harsh and severe forms of physical treatment, like cold baths, electric shock treatment and straightjackets were normal. The group felt that there must be other more humane methods to try and understand the nature of what they knew as the 'functional nervous diseases'. It was agreed to concentrate on hysteria, a common illness among the female patients. The group recognised that the hysteria originated from inner states of dysfunction, disturbing internal mental activities, from an unknown source of the nervous system. Consequently, the decision was to find a less hostile means to deviate from those harsh methods and find a more humane form of treatment.

Originally, this group felt that mental problems could be understood from a philosophical stance. Soon after some of the professionals split from the original group stating that they thought this approach was unscientific and searched for a more specialised form of treatment. Diversifying from the previous treatment, the split-off group decided to concentrate on hypnosis, a method already used by a few. This small group, including Sigmund Freud and Joseph Breuer, met regularly to discuss their findings and thoughts on the new mode of treatment. Some of them noted that the patients were displaying some behavioural patterns whilst under hypnosis.

Joseph Breuer noted that a young woman, whom he was treating for hysteria, acted out some behaviour of a sexual nature whilst under hypnosis. When she had come out of the hypnotic state he tentatively alluded to what he thought had happened without being accusative. She admitted that she had sexual desires towards her father. They arose from the past, at a time when she was nursing him through an illness. Those desires and feelings continued to disturb her. Realising that this was probably the cause of her hysteria, he made her aware that her repressed feelings were the basis of her illness. Surprisingly, he soon discovered that she was not only listening, but responded to some of what he said. Progressively, as her trust in him grew, she divulged some of her intimate feelings and thoughts. Simultaneously her hysterics became less evident and he noted that her condition improved. Finding that someone was prepared to listen to her without criticism encouraged her to reveal more of her phantasies and desires. As their meetings progressed, the more she trusted him the more she divulged about her innermost feelings and thoughts.

By using the same approach with other patients, Breuer decided that their respective neurosis stemmed from impulses that were too disturbing to think about, let alone act upon. The inadmissible feelings remained as mental activities because they were mostly not permissible. Those unwanted, internalised, repressed feelings manifested externally as hysteria. Until he gently pointed out some of their yearnings, the patients were not consciously aware of their non-verbalised feelings. He continued to work through hypnosis, followed by talking to his patients about some of his thoughts. He encouraged his patients to speak about their feelings, which helped them to recall and remember what they might have felt as previously unspeakable. Gradually, he concluded that hysteria had replaced the impulses that could not be acted upon for various reasons. Not only acknowledging but admitting to what they felt for the first time improved their mental condition. Breuer continued to use this technique as a mode of treatment, noting that their mental states improved. Realistically, this was a great step forward in the treatment of hysteria, Breuer however, hesitant about his findings, kept his discovery to himself. Others continued with the method of hypnosis but failed to come to any conclusive thoughts or findings. Why Breuer did not share his significant discovery is not clear. Perhaps he felt his mode of treatment was unscientific.

Almost fifteen years later, Breuer tentatively shared his thoughts with his colleague, Freud. After much discussion and collaboration, they concluded that the desired impulses were repressed and outwardly manifested as hysteria. The impulses and associated feelings remained in the psyche because they could not be acted upon as societal values prohibited that kind of behaviour. Frustration of those unfulfilled desires became unbearable. This persuaded Breuer, perhaps with support from Freud, to establish that the powerful existence of the reality that could not be acted upon or spoken about, remained internalised, causing painful, unbearable mental states or physical illnesses. Their secrets became a part of their 'inner state' resulting in an outer display of hysteria. Freud and Breuer together discerned and established that hysteria, which was previously acknowledged as coming from physiological, nervous disorders, was, in fact, the incapacity to hold unwanted, undesired mental feelings. Hysteria was the outer display of inner unprocessed yearnings causing frustrations. Together, they published their findings, *Studies on Hysteria* (1895d). Freud later wrote a further paper on the subject after his work with several other patients. The discovery was the turning point in the treatment of hysteria. Soon after, for some unknown reason, Breuer discontinued treating hysterical patients to return to work as a medical consultant.

Freud, from thereon, encouraged his patients to speak about anything that came to mind including their feelings about their illness. He keenly listened to them while they 'free associated' their thoughts as their trust in him grew. By his uncritical approach they trusted him and revealed more and more of their innermost feelings and thoughts as never before. Much of this at first came over as confused and difficult to understand. But he persisted with this new technique. Diversifying from his original training as a neurosurgeon, he devoted his studies on the internal world and the part it played on the lives of people until his death. During his early work with emotionally dysfunctional females, he made copious notes of their symptoms, reactions and nuances. The more they trusted him the more they revealed. Their secretive thoughts and desires were no longer 'buried secrets' and their mental states improved. In some cases, the hysteria had altogether disappeared. Seeing him regularly enabled a trusting relationship and the patients revealed aspects of their personal feelings as they had never previously verbalised to anyone or even acknowledged to themselves. Relieved of these burdensome disturbances, they gradually learnt to accept their unwanted feelings and integrate them as part of their personality. This resulted in alleviating their mental stress. Hence, the treatment is now, at times, still referred to as the 'talking cure'.

He restricted the meetings to fifty-minutes sessions, presumably giving himself ten minutes of the hour allocated to each patient, to make copious notes. Currently, psychotherapists continue to use this time limit. The meticulous notes he had collated soon after seeing patients enabled Freud to religiously study and establish what he considered was the cause of their problems. He discovered that most of their hysteria was linked to those unspoken, internalised feelings. He also noted that those original feelings and thoughts remained with them and could not be rid of. They were recalled and remembered without prompting. By methodically comparing repetitive incidents in relation to when, why and how these symptoms began, he came to some grounded theories. He concluded that their unspoken secrets and longings, which could not be acted upon, or talked about for various ethical reasons, remained repressed internally and manifested in the outer state as hysteria and/or other physical illnesses. This led him to believe that every feeling or experience of our lifetime remained in the psyche or 'inner self' and only temporarily lost to the conscious self. He concluded that unbearable, painful, adverse experiences cannot be annihilated. Involuntarily they are repressed in the psyche and remain as 'unconscious processes'. Developmentally, this was the paradigm of the existence of the 'unconscious', which led him to believe that every experience remained in this 'storeroom' as 'unconscious processes'. He further posited that at any given moment a past experience may be triggered off during the present without any deliberate prodding. His discovery was the genesis of the unconscious, we now not only accept but take for granted.

For various reasons we may ignore, forget or lose through trauma some or most of our past experiences as discussed in Chapter 9. Freud also pointed out that certain feelings and longings cannot be acted upon or spoken of openly, like those of his hysterical patients. No form of external physical treatment or medication healed their internal states. Medication does not heal states of stress, anxiety or depression. It helps to temporarily control the state of mind. Talking about distressing thoughts to someone that can be trusted helps to relieve the burden as it is no longer repressed/suppressed. Freud thus pioneered the 'talking cure'. His discovery was the turning point of the study of our inner world, known as psychoanalysis/psychotherapy.

Freud went on to theorise that our mental functioning involved three stages: 'notation, judgement and action'. He concluded that at any given moment a 'notation', originating and transmitted through the senses instigates the thought process. Thinking about it is necessary before a 'judgement' is made, followed by the appropriate 'action'.

Simply, when we have a feeling, we should note and think about what it entails before acting upon it. In other words all our actions are the result of the judgement we make, from those feelings that come from internal processes.

For example: the feeling of love is usually expressed more readily but there are times when it may not be appropriate to convey for various reasons. You cannot help falling in love with a married colleague or boss, your best friend's partner or someone unsuitable. By thinking about it, you realise that you have no control over the experience but the action decided upon is your responsibility. You make the choice. Through quick processing you make the decision to keep the feeling to yourself or tell the person involved. You have not denied the experience. Societal and moral values play a significant role and affect how we react to some of our feelings.

As a pioneer, Freud influenced colleagues and other professionals working in the field of mental dysfunctional states. He recognised that most outer activities and behaviour resulted from the decisions we make, originated from internal, intra-psychic sources we have no control over. Every experience of one's lifetime remains within us. Early experiences that took place during our nurturing years may be activated at any given moment, resulting in happy feelings or distress. As noted in the chapter on memory, some may be correctly remembered, others in a confused state or totally forgotten. He verified that the mind directs and coordinates the other areas devoted to fulfilling instincts, needs and fundamental drives. Much of his literature on the subject is still respected as the embodiment of understanding the unconscious.

Freud spent almost his entire working lifetime sketching a theoretical framework to determine that the study of psychoanalysis was a natural science. But the scientific status of psychoanalysis is still equivocal. Some consider it as being in the category of the humanities. Although his legacy is continued to be acknowledged in its original form by a small circle of followers, some of his contributions are now refuted. Others have been expanded upon, posited or amalgamated with further themes from other contributors. Nevertheless, he introduced a more humane form of treatment and a new process of thinking about mental disorders. He also established the existence of the unconscious and the significant role it plays on our daily lives. This humane form of treatment invariably works as it is still in practise almost two centuries later.

Carl Jung was originally an enthusiast of Freud's methodology. He initially accepted Freud's concepts but later differed and disputed some of his theories. His analytic psychology posited the central theme as individuation, elaborating on the process of integrating the opposites – namely the conscious with the unconscious – while maintaining their relative autonomy. Jung later went on to consider individuation involving archetypes and collective unconscious to be the central process of human development. Human aesthetic experiences are explained as the microcosm of the universal macrocosm. Both Freud and Jung contributed in specific ways towards the rethinking of treatment for mental re-figuration and integration to achieve a state of equilibrium. Other schools of developmental psychology pertaining to the linking and working on unconscious processes are now in practice. During the twentieth century, two psychiatrists, Oliver Sachs and Ronald Laing, played significant roles in creating awareness that institutionalism was not the appropriate answer for all mental illnesses.

Listening and observing during a psychotherapeutic session

Two very vital concepts play an important role in the part of the psychotherapist; as repeatedly stressed, the capacity to listen intently and to observe. Essentially, the practice of psychotherapeutic work is based on intellectual knowledge and understanding of the theoretical concepts learnt during training, together with one's own intense analysis to personally understand experiential activities. The training enables the psychotherapist to listen and observe without confusing one's own feelings and thoughts with those of the patient. Trust plays a significant role as the patient must feel assured that whatever he says remains confidential. It requires the ability to translate what is going on or happening in the 'inner state' of the patient. As seen by the stories in Section One, and the excerpts and vignettes that follow in Section Two, there are manifold reasons as to why one receives therapy. People come for therapy for various reasons linked with uncomfortable states of mind. These include feelings of anxiety, distress, unhappiness, panic, not being able to make relationships, bereavement. The list is endless. Some come of their own accord or are referred by professionals and clinicians. They want to be relieved of troublesome feelings and find some meaning as to why this is happening to them. Some are referred because their doctors cannot find any physical reason for their ill health. Others are depressed or extremely anxious.

The non-judgemental, non-critical, non-advisory role of the psychotherapist provides a space for the person seeking help to think over intimate, personal, undesirable thoughts and feelings that have been troublesome or persecuting. As trust develops and more is revealed, exposure and rethinking and reorganising one's state of mind brings about relief. The original feelings are never erased. Toleration and understanding of them helps to alleviate pain. Patients make their own decisions about aspects of their life that had been previously incomprehensible. Undoubtedly, honesty plays an important role and it is not altogether easy to confess and be open about some unsavoury thoughts. Simultaneously, one cannot accept everything as the *pure truth* because with the passing of time, some experiences may have become blurred, distorted or confused. However, in my thinking, if an earlier experience, which may not be truthful in its entirety due to confusion, does prevent one from living a contented lifestyle, then one should accept this to move on. Obviously, one needs to be cautious when it comes to false accusations and confrontation. Seeking revenge against innocent people is not the way to move forward.

The role of the psychotherapist is to encourage the client to create a way of life by negotiating and integrating unwanted experiences. It is necessary to once more stress that the psychotherapist does not deliberately suggest how one should change. The patient/client learns to do this as a way of life. As mentioned earlier, unwanted feelings can never be rid of but can be accepted for what they represent, forego and move forward. In my experience, when this is achieved then psychotherapy has brought relief and emotional well-being to those people. It is also essential to say that psychotherapeutic intervention is not a miraculous activity that automatically results in successful changes. One must be prepared to consider every aspect of one's negative behaviour and sincerely consider what changes are necessary to improve one's self. Some feel incapable of doing this for various reasons. Confronting the truth can be emotionally painful or the traumatised memory cannot cope with negative aspects of the self. Psychotherapy encourages one to create a lifestyle and attain a way of life, by looking into and studying oneself from a critical stance to attain a personality or individuality.

The following stories may help to create some awareness of whether psychotherapeutic intervention was helpful or not. Perhaps those who have been reluctant to seek help will be encouraged to come knowing what to expect. Also bearing in mind that psychotherapy can be beneficial by making changes for the better and improving one's emotional well-being for the future. Everyone, including Freud, probably had feelings that were repressed. It would be preferable to work through many of the repressed feelings and come to some understanding, rather than feel silently haunted or ill.

* * *

Robbie, at forty-three, was intelligent and well established in a lucrative career, but had difficulties in his relationships with women. Both his younger brother and sister seemed happy with their partners and children. He visited them frequently, adored his nephews and nieces, and lavished them with expensive presents. Often, he would come to a meeting looking very excited. He could not wait to tell me the good news. He had met another 'gorgeous woman'. She was the one for him. Not long after, I was not surprised that the relationship had ended. I soon discovered that this was the pattern as his relationships did not last for long. It seemed to me that Robbie was looking for someone special, an 'idealised, perfect woman'.

One day, he came in looking very distraught and angry. He refused to say anything. I observed him twitching and shaking his head. This made me ask what was wrong, adding that perhaps something unacceptable had happened. Angrily, he replied, "My stupid mother has decided to get married for the third time! Why now! Why not remain as friends like they have been? She is doing a SKI!" (I discovered later this abbreviation meant Spending the Kids Inheritance). This was followed by a prolonged silence.

Eventually, I gathered that his mother, who was in her early seventies, had decided to marry her neighbour. He had become a widower about five years before and often helped his mother with various chores. What neither Robbie nor his siblings had guessed was that more was going on between them. This was her third relationship. His father deserted them for another woman when Robbie was twelve and being the eldest he had felt responsible for his mother. He imagined himself to be the 'man of the house' and it was his responsibility in phantasy to take care of his mother/partner and his younger siblings. His mother, unknown to him, had had a relationship when he was at university with someone who travelled a lot and was not a permanent feature. A few months after he finished his course and moved back, he found out about the relationship.

At that point, he was seeing a girl he had met at university. His mother invited him and his girlfriend to dinner, when she announced the news of her intended marriage to that partner. His siblings were delighted, but he had to pretend to be so. He divulged that he felt furious at the time. That relationship lasted a couple of years before they divorced amicably. By then Robbie had drifted from one relationship to another. He now hardly visited his mother, except when necessary. Quite unexpectedly she announced her current plans to marry again.

"Why marry? Why marry again at her age?" he yelled, angrily thumping the couch with his right hand.

Leading on from this, he confided how much he hated seeing his brother and sister 'play the happy family' when he visited. He then quickly explained, "I do really love them all, you know."

It took many months of working together to understand and connect his feelings to his past experiences and phantasies. His mother had been devastated by the loss of her first husband when he had left. Emotionally vulnerable, she had turned to her children for love and comfort. Psychologically, he became his mother's partner. The excitement of university and the beginnings of a new lifestyle seemed normal. As an older adolescent and young adult, Robbie associated with several women of his age, but the relationships never lasted for long. Although not consciously thought about, there was no woman who could compare with his mother. It took months of therapy to work through the anger, guilt and envy before he could accept his mother's decision to remarry.

The negative effect of experiences with parents – through no deliberate actions from either party – may impact upon later relationships. During childhood and early adolescence, many varied kinds of daily activities impact on an individual. Many survive all kinds of detrimental experiences and live satisfactory lifestyles. Some young people are affected in the most unexpected ways. Sadly, Robbie could never shift from his state of mind. Intellectually, he understood what I conveyed to him, but he could not change emotionally. Like some people, he could not make the mental plunge and realistically confront his feelings. He carried this negative state of mind with him, afraid to let go. Unfortunately, he was internally stuck as being his mother's protector and partner.

On a more positive note, the following story has a pleasant ending. Sandy, twenty-three, returned from her job abroad as a voluntary worker at a war camp in Africa. She was the fourth child of six, consisting of three boys and three girls. Her mother had run away with her four young children from an abusive, alcoholic partner. The two older children, who were already in a home run by nuns, remained there. Sandy did not know her father as she was about three when this happened. He had totally disappeared from her life. They lived in a garage that had been converted into simple living accommodation. However, she could recall there being a 'Daddy' around all through childhood. When Sandy was nearly eleven, her mother became seriously ill and the children were sent to a Christian charity home run by nuns. At the age of eleven, she and her two brothers were fostered by a childless couple who later adopted all three of them. The older sister of the four remained with the foster parents until she started working soon after. They hardly saw her as she lived a long way off. Sandy and her brothers were given a good education and Sandy felt she was loved. She maintained a warm relationship with her adopted parents. She and her brothers looked upon them as loving parents. Whenever possible, they visited or stayed with them. She related that it was like going back home.

Sandy had been given long-term leave because she was suffering from stress and staying with her adoptive parents. She said she was enjoying being spoilt. It was a real treat after camp life. Her own mother, suffering from poor health, had returned to her home town to live with a sister. Sandy's adopted mother suggested she seek support for her stress and was paying for her therapy.

To begin with, after gaining two good grades in her 'A' levels, Sandy went backpacking around the Far East with the aim of helping to educate poor village children. Intermittently, she and an American girl, Rita, with whom she became friendly, toured the big cities and worked at the large hotels to earn money to pay for their trips. After nearly two years of really enjoying this lifestyle, she helped at a spa. She met an American tourist, whom she became infatuated with. He was on his own and there for a fortnight. Becoming emotional she eventually volunteered, "I can't forgive myself. How stupid of me! I despised my mother for her promiscuous lifestyle and hated her for it. I was not going to be like her and sleep with the first man who charmed me with his lies!"

It transpired that she spent a whole week with the American, who promised to keep in touch and invited her to visit him. He gave her an address and telephone number. Not long after he left, she and Rita returned to their village. To her horror, she realised that she was pregnant. Her initial thinking was to contact the American. She was shocked to discover that he had given a false address and phone number. She was in a dilemma as to whether she should have the baby or not. Overwhelming thoughts of her mother came to the fore. After some contemplation with the help of a village woman, she drank a concoction that brought on a heavy menstruation, leaving her feeling sick and very weak.

"It was an experience that I would not wish on anyone! I thought I was going to die. I now feel horrified when I think about the risk. It could have been the end of me. The bleeding went on and on and eventually the wife of the village head who ran the school took me to a doctor. He gave me an injection and some tablets that helped. I promised myself I would never trust another man."

After her horrific experience, which she seemed to have coped with, she continued to train and became an aid worker. Her aim had always been to help deprived children. She worked incessantly and she felt that this was the cause of her stressful state. Her condition seemed to have started recently. After many weeks she hesitantly referred to a co-worker who was very keen on her. She was very fond of him. She tried not to get into an intimate relationship with him. She felt attracted to him, but also confused. Her worrying led to sleepless nights. She did not want to lose him and declining to become intimate with him was creating problems.

Recently, the urge to get to know and renew her relationship with her eldest sister, older brother and especially her sick mother continually came to mind. She had not seen them for some time. She hardly knew her two older siblings. Her mother must have loved her but could not help getting ill. She felt that worrying about all that made her feel stressed. Thoughts about her childhood also kept her awake. She recalled that during her childhood, her mother had often been unwell and had stayed in bed. The sister who was older than her took care of her and the two younger brothers. She vaguely recalled some of the rows between her mother and the man who lived with them. When he punched her mother, she used to cringe in the corner with pain as if they were directed at her. Much to her relief, he eventually left and none of them ever saw him again. She now thought of her mother as a weak-minded, sickly woman, who could not stand up to the men in her life. Often when in close contact with the frightened children and the victims of war that she came across in her work, memories of her past were recalled. She was determined that she was not going to be like her mother and let men ruin her life.

"I will never forgive myself for letting that American play such a nasty trick on me. It was really abuse. I will never let it happen again." She never used his name. He was always referred to as the American.

This information made me wonder about her relationship with the person at the camp she intermittently referred to. I tentatively suggested that perhaps she was judging all men by the behaviour of the American. Maybe that was her reason for not getting too close to her friend at the camp whom she liked. She did not respond but I felt that had impacted on her. She remained silent, a bit unusual for her. After a long pause she volunteered that she liked him a lot. He was a very caring person.

Sandy came for almost six months. She felt a lot better within herself and returned to her workplace abroad. During her therapy, she recalled and remembered a fair amount of her childhood. She had experienced some shattering, painful experiences. The mother becoming ill and her having to be fostered was a godsend. For example, the mother, when feeling too ill, was unable to care for them. Often, during those times, there was no food or money. The mother used to go out cleaning a few homes whenever she could. The older sister used to take them to the local street market at closing

----

time. They picked up anything that was edible and that was to be their supper on some days. If they were lucky a stall keeper gave them some of the left overs. She recalled how often she awoke in the middle of the night feeling very hungry. When the mother felt a little better she used to make a huge pot of stew. This was to be their meal for several days. If one could string together negative experiences to wear as a necklace then Sandy's childhood allowed for that to be possible. Her early years were one of poverty, deprivation, neglect and emotional abuse. One dreads to think about what could have happened to Sandy and her siblings. They were lucky to be adopted by two loving, nurturing adults who helped to keep the nightmares at bay. Thereafter, she always stayed with them when back from her various postings. Her younger siblings also kept close contact with them.

I would like to add that these feelings sound a little idolised. I will never know the truth. They were probably good parents as they did not have children of their own. Sandy's mother was a very needy woman, deprived of love. She was often physically ill. It was not that she did not love her children, but she was unable to take care of them. Sandy could see this and learnt not to blame her mother, which led to her decision to visit her. With the help of her adopted parents, she arranged a family reunion. When I last heard from her, she was in a relationship with her co-worker. He sounded like a caring person and they planned to move to another placement together.

Psychotherapy today

Although the practise of psychoanalysis/psychotherapy has taken several directions since it was first inaugurated by Sigmund Freud, it has survived over two centuries. Currently, there are different orientations by new schools of thinking, combining a philosophical, religious approach or quick-fix methods of gaining access into 'unconscious processes'. Critics have discarded and reconstructed some of the original theories as false and have introduced new themes. Essentially it is the process of healing emotional anxieties and depression. However, the main schools of training have remained with the in-depth methodology, which entails many years of intense training to work with patients. It is still, perhaps, the only means of understanding psychic phenomena and emotional disorders.

In practice, psychoanalytic and psychotherapeutic interventions are closely akin. The only major difference is the training. The former requirement is for two patients to be seen five times weekly during the training period. Three to five times weekly is acceptable for training as a psychotherapist by the major teaching institutions. The theoretical literature for both trainings is basically similar. Many clinicians adapt their working method to suit their workplace. In the NHS psychotherapeutic intervention is usually limited to once weekly for a period of one year. Some now offer an even shorter span of treatment.

Almost every clinician will agree that working as a psychotherapist is mentally exhausting. One spends one's working hours like a sponge, mopping up a host of feelings, mostly negative, of anxiety, anger, despair, distress, guilt, perversity, phantasy, mental pain and occasionally happy, pleasurable emotions. Analysing the material involves careful listening and observation of the patient's nuances. This enables some understanding of the patient's emotional state, often to do with negative activities of the personality.

Recalling, remembering and integrating

Recalling and remembering are predominantly uncontrollable states of mind. Daily, we deliberately recall from memory. At other times remembrance of things past come to mind without us making any effort or prompting. During psychotherapy one recollection may lead to other remembrances from the past. The practice is about looking into earlier dysfunctional 'object relations' by encouraging 'free associations' during the session. Undesirable and painful experiences can be worked through with the 'new object' – the analyst. The original experience or feelings such as anger, hate and fear, within the facilitating environment of the consulting room are often recalled as one thought leads to other connected ones. Often those childhood experiences that were intolerable become emotionally bearable by the holding and understanding of those feelings by the analyst.

It takes some time before the patient trusts the psychotherapist. At the beginning, there may be reluctance to recall or divulge what is recalled. Unfortunately, as earlier discussed, this can cause emotional distress to varying degrees. The aim of the analyst or psychotherapist is to encourage the recalling and remembering. Evasion of psychic pain unfortunately prevents many from talking openly about themselves. Some manage to do this immediately, while others remain too afraid or reluctant to recall and remember unsavoury experiences. They develop a shell or hard crust that may be impenetrable.

Temporarily, the psychotherapist may be a replacement for anyone involved – mother, father, a sibling or any other figure of authority – at the time. The sex or age of the surrogate object makes no difference. The raw feelings are once more experienced and may be 'acted out' in the consulting room. Some patients tend to 'act out' with partners, close members of the family or friends. It can be better contained during a session as the therapist is trained to deal with this kind of behaviour. No professional, no matter how experienced, can help to bring about positive changes without the genuine participation and motivation of the recipient. I repeat, the analyst only acts as a catalyst. Some changes may be initiated.

Psychotherapy is not a magic form of cure. It is hard work and painful to re-evoke, re-explore and experience previously unwanted, negative feelings, which were originally too painful to accept. The raw experience may still be indigestible and may remain as such. Psychotherapy does not work if the recipient continually resists and refuses to let go of the past. It is then not a suitable form of treatment and fails to bring about changes. As repeatedly stressed, the past is very much the present as well as the future. Most people prefer to ignore or try to dispose of undesirable states of mind. A balanced state of mind can only be achieved if one critically looks at one's negative behaviour as this does not automatically disappear, except in exceptional cases.

It is necessary to stress that talking to a family member or a friend may relieve some pain, but for integration and successful restoration of the psyche, the skill of the psychotherapist is required. The capacity to recognise and interpret the underlying meaning, re-experience the pain and accept it as part of one's legacy is necessary before any healing can take place. The client's anecdotes are often connected with their past life. The troublesome feelings and thoughts may have lingered somewhere vaguely in the background but may not be identifiable. They may quite suddenly become significant or clarify other connected behavioural experiences. Remembering undesirable feelings from one's past not only stirs up painful feelings, but some memorable ones as well. During the therapy, a wide range of feelings of guilt, hate, rejection, jealousy, envy and anger are generally stirred up. The negative feelings are shelved or denied instead of being confronted and accepted in their raw state. By denying the reality of these unwanted experiences, the person concerned can remain in a pleasurable state of mind. The therapeutic space allows for such feelings to be expressed or re-experienced. This allows for integration, instead of avoidance and repression. Although recollection of unsavoury past experiences may once more be felt with the past associated pain, they are openly shared without shame. Generally people are reluctant to speak about any activities thought to be shameful. But as their trust in the person-centred, confidential environment of the consulting room develops, they more readily do so.

However, psychotherapy is not the answer for everyone. Some people may need medication to alleviate their stressful or depressing states of mind. It may not be useful if the diagnosis indicates organic dysfunction or they are too traumatised and vulnerable to be exposed to such stress. For those with milder forms of emotional disturbances, medication alleviates the condition but does not get to the root of the problem. Depression and stress can be linked with states of mind or a part of the psyche being in stasis. Before launching into the therapeutic experience, an individual must be genuinely prepared to be honest with himself and his therapist. As earlier discussed, it is commonly known as a 'talking cure'.

What is related in the consulting room may come under a 'false memory syndrome' and be far from the truth. But if the patient believes that it is his experience causing him such distress, then there can be no harm done if he finds relief to unburden himself. One has to separate what is his truth from that of falsely accusing or blaming anyone else. Psychotherapy treatment is not a quick fix. Trust is a relevant factor that needs to develop between client and analyst for the treatment to be successful. Some intense work may relieve some people of some stressful states of mind within a few months and this may be all they need. Others with in-depth problems may require a longer timespan before the therapy helps. For successful results, grieving, mourning and remorse are definitive requirements. Psychotherapy can become a way of life even long after one has finished having sessions. It is also invasive in that it trains the recipient to observe, scrutinise and distinguish one's behaviour. Psychotherapy cultivates a mental state of awareness as observation skills become keener when one begins to see everyday life events more realistically. The benefits continue after the therapy has ended because one has learnt to scrutinise one's behaviour patterns and daily experiences, think about them and deal with them as appropriate, rather than deny them.

Therapeutic intervention is not based on logical and intellectual facts, but by understanding experiential information that may not always be the truth. A non-judgemental perspective is maintained. Accusations are considered and left to the discretion of the patient to integrate whenever possible. The psychotherapist is cautious with patients who have a tendency or want to blame others. Whatever the complaint, it must be understood for what it means to the patient and worked with accordingly. Secrets and lies may be distorted, accusative or just disturbing. Psychotherapists are just as infallible as other clinicians and professionals. Working with vulnerable people who trust you requires care and precaution as to how one is with them. In a nutshell, psychotherapy cultivates a sincere way of life. It is about finding one's true self by differentiating between thoughts that come from 'I' to those from 'me' as Proust indicated.

12

FURTHER THOUGHTS

It can also be argued that long before Freud stereotyped psychoanalysis, an awareness of 'unconscious processes' was in existence from ancient times. The witch doctors of Africa and South America, crows of North America, swamis, gurus, fakirs in India and the shamans of Scandinavia, to name a few, were already relieving people of psychic pain or supporting them of stressful feelings to acquire emotional equilibrium. The soul or spirit was considered as the seat of the inner psychic world, now referred to as the self in the analytic world. During those days and no different to the present, there were quacks claiming they could help. The study of psychoanalysis is also considered from a theoretical perspective to encourage positive behavioural patterns of thinking. This kind of approach probably helps some traumatised people.

As previously stated my aim is to open the subject of psychotherapy to a wider, lay readership without making it 'pop psychology'. This can only be done by explaining the existence of the 'unconscious' that Freud bequeathed to us in the twentieth century. We now take this for granted. It is difficult to imagine that the word 'unconscious' conveys a very active, internal world, never thought about before

Freud introduced its existence and the major role it plays during our everyday lifetime. Also relevant is that Freud's philosophy of the 'existence of the unconscious' created an entirely new form of thinking about human behaviour. Although there are not all that many practitioners closely following Freud's original theories and methodology of working, any form of psychotherapeutic intervention stems from Freud's pioneering and original thinking.

Schools of other humane origins, like incorporating a hermeneutic approach, philosophical and behavioural psychology, spiritualism or other forms of treatment using academic knowledge does not qualify one to practise as a psychotherapist. The framework of psychoanalytic theory is, perhaps, difficult to understand, but the person who comes to therapy does not need to know any of this. The involved, intricate, learned theory is doubtless constantly in the mind of the psychotherapist. This knowledge is essential to try and understand what is going on in the mind of the patient. The therapist does not inform or direct a person to behave in any manner, nor act like a teacher, be accusative towards the patient or of anyone he refers to in a derogative manner. It is a humane form of activity and often one strand of thought leads to another. It is a way of making the patient think and consider how he can make changes to improve his life. It encourages the patient to develop an honest and sincere perspective of himself. This way of considering himself promotes him to achieving his own individuality. For long after the therapy ends his improved way of thinking and behaviour continues. His ability and skills to listen and observer as an instinctive part of his daily life, enhances his lifestyle. Facing the truth is not altogether conducive for various reasons. Some people with chronic ailments live for their problem, which has become part of their lifeline. If curtailed of it, they will perish or vegetate. Friends cannot or do not always understand the inner functioning and may only be able to support one to a peripheral extent. For others, swallowing a readily available tablet may be preferable.

As previously discussed, scepticism and reluctance to accept psychological therapeutic interventions is probably due to the stigma still attached to emotional and mental disorders. Many people feel like a failure if they need to go to therapy to sort out their problems. Others who undergo the treatment recognise the benefit but are reluctant to tell others that they are seeing a therapist. For many, the initial meeting is looked upon with trepidation. However, once one is in the consulting room, it often feels different to what one imagined. Sorting out one's life is similar, in some respects, to finding the various pieces of a jigsaw puzzle to create a whole picture. Put simply, the patient learns ways of coping with personal difficulties and function more productively during daily activities. It is, however, relevant to note that painful feelings are stirred up during therapy, but this, in turn, leads to a more productive lifestyle once the truth is accepted for what it is. Working through unwanted parts of the self may be an incentive and lead to achieve aspirations and creativity, before only imagined to be possible.

During psychotherapy, talking is the main form of communication, but patients may use bodily nuances to convey some of their feelings. For example, a patient feeling vulnerable as associations of childhood experiences are related may curl up in a foetal position or make sounds related to an infant. The facilitating environment encourages certain behaviour to be acted during the session, but this does not mean that the patient demonstrates irresponsible, undesirable or dangerous types of behaviour. Through training and experience, the therapist is one step ahead of the patient and prevents such situations from arising. Unwelcome behaviour is talked about rather than acted upon. The supportive role of the psychotherapist as an object mainly helps the adult to express his feelings through the medium of language. In the 'transference situation' the therapist may temporarily represent mother, father, partner or the other. Having said that, there are times when silence can be just as meaningful in indicating what the patient is feeling.

These pages only cover a very small part of the practice. Our dream world has not been touched upon. Psychotherapists, yet again influenced by Freud, interpret dreams. It is believed that our dreams tell us an immense amount of our inner life. It is understood that we dream almost nightly. We mostly forget them, but significant ones often reoccur and are eventually remembered. If noted keenly, we can learn a lot more about our emotional states through dreams. Freud wrote a whole volume on *The Interpretation of Dreams* (1899). It is recognised that when one is in therapy, one dreams more often, remembering and noting them.

Finally, I believe that our experiences are unique to us whether they be pleasurable or troublesome. We should not only accept the pleasant ones but consider the undesirable ones for what they represent. We cannot change our past experiences, but we can improve our future although there may be many hurdles and difficulties before this may be achieved. After giving our undesirable activities some thought, we should learn to mourn our losses. If we have suffered cruelly, then for the sake of our own improvement, try to practise my three favourite words, which are; 'Forego, Forgive and move Forward'. I feel that only then we can improve our inner state and move on to an improved emotional lifestyle. Psychotherapy can support to heal and achieve a new improved personality.

CONCLUSION

I would like to include a poem written by Tristan Williams, in memory of his grandfather, Dr Arthur Hyatt Williams. I feel immense gratitude towards the late Dr Williams who, throughout my training, especially in a supervisory role, impacted on how I worked as a clinician. He encouraged me to be myself without blurring the boundaries with my patient. As a keen follower of Wilfred Bion, he not only followed his philosophy of learning from one's experience, he influenced me to think in a similar way. Under his jovial manner, his great sense of humour and his intermittent anecdotes of past experiences, there was a sensitive, sincere and deeply intuitive man. From him, I learnt to pay attention to the past and acknowledge it without remaining in stasis there. Nor do I expect that the future will give me what I desire, but to concentrate on the present and, most importantly of all, to be true to myself.

Oh, how I have lived

As I lie here,
Helpless as a tot,
Fading like paper in the sun,
Incapable of opening my eyes to the morning,
Or a door to a pretty girl,
Or even a jar of jam.

Stroke my hair,
And feel my pity,
For I have lived.
Oh, how I have lived.

As a boy
Leaping two footed into the world.
Sharp as vinegar keen as mustard
Kissing frogs and scoffing hedgehogs.
Drinking in days that lasted years,
And years that last twice the length.
Regularly voyaging to the ends of the earth,
And back again in time for tea.

As a soldier:
Burma bound; Birkenhead bred.
Brown as toast.
Reading Hemingway in the jungle:
Death in the afternoon
Death in the morning
Death for tea.
And all an adventure for me.

As a doctor:
Shepherding the mind,
Of the mad,
Fishing for clues in that vast ocean.
Somehow holding them afloat:
A steady rock for the storm-wrecked sailor to cling to.

As a father:
Act 1 : Sons.
And plenty of them.
Strict but fair.

Whipping boys for whipping apples,
And saving Bill from the angry mob.
Act 2 : Daughters.
An alien race,
But fairer of face,
And through them, out came the fairer in me.
I did my best,
They did the rest.

As a husband:
Good as gold,
And happy as Larry,
Most of the time.
Oh ye capricious Gods!
Widowing me twice,
Marrying me thrice,
But loving them all the same.

As a grandfather:
Flitting between flowers of exquisite beauty,
(So I am told)
Like a butterfly.
Pollinating young minds.
Trading stories like trading punches.
Happiest of all when introducing a friend or two:
The Brimstone, the Orange Tip, The Pearl-bordered Fritillary,
The tricky obin, La Belle Dame and the Doomed Youth.

As a man:
Where to begin?
So infinite in faculties and wisdom;
So abhorred of TV,
And the J-cloth,
And keeping to the speed limit.

No truer gentleman Jim.
Sharp as a new pin
Fizzing with zest for life's tonic and gin.

And so it ends,
As it does,
Without reason,
Or rhyme.
No Hollywood ending this time.
It is the long goodbye for me,
And that's fine.
Just fine.

So long then scattered Barton and the holy Tuscan sun,
Those Eastern Isles and the rare Pelistry.
Each and every garden bee that has helped me, and my farmers
Brown.
And of course, those early hours I know so well.
Goodbye.

And now you see,
Feel no sorrow for me,
Just stroke my hair,
Kiss me,
And smile.
For now you know I have lived
Oh, how I have lived.

Tristan Williams

REFERENCES AND FURTHER READING:

1. Sigmund Freud: 1905a, *On Psychotherapy*
    Std. Ed. 7: 257-268; London, Hogarth
    - 1908, *Some General Remarks on Hysterical Attacks*
      Std. Ed. 9: London, Hogarth
    - 1915, *On Metapsychology*
      Std. Ed. 11: 167-173: London Hogarth

2. Freud & Breuer: 1895d, *Studies on Hysteria*. Freud & Breuer: Std. Ed 2, 3-51 London Hogarth

3. Melanie Klein: 1946, *Notes on Some Interior Mechanisms, Envy and Gratitude & Other Works*, Vol 1: 1-24: London, Karnac Books
    - 1952, *The Origins of Transference, Envy and Gratitude & Other Works*, Vol. 1: 8-56: London, Karnac Books
    - 1959, *Our Adult World and its Roots in Infancy, Envy and Gratitude and Other Works*, Vol 1: 247-263: London, Karnac Books

4. Wilfred Bion: 1991 *Learning from Experience*, London, Karnac Books: (First Published: 1962 by London Heinemann) 1993

Second Thoughts: Commentary 120–186, London, Karnac Books: (First Published: 1967 by London, Heinemann)

5. Esther Bick: 1964 *Notes on Infant Observation in Psychoanalytic Training, Int. Journal of Psychoanalysis*: 45: 484-488

6. John Bowlby: 1980, *Psychoanalysis as a Natural Science: Freud Memorial Inaugural Lectures*: University College London

7. Michael Rustin: 2002, *Looking in the right place: complexity theory, psychoanalysis and infant observation, Int. Journal of Infant Observation and its' Applications*, Vol. 5, No 1

Other References

Marcel Proust, *Remembrance of Things Past*, translated by Scott Moncrieff.
Bernard Levin, *Unnamed Poem on Shakespeare*, (see Wikipedia)
William Blake, *Songs of Innocence and Experience*, (1789) (1794)

ACKNOWLEDGEMENTS

My special thanks to Prof Michael Rustin for his consistent encouragement as my academic supervisor. Sincerely thankful to Sheila Miller, as tutor, clinical supervisor and her keen interest in all my professional work, as well as remaining a good friend. This is also an opportunity to say thank you to Prof Andrew Cooper, for his support with my thesis related to psychotherapeutic work with older adults as well as Margaret Rustin and Gianna Williams who intermittently played an influential role in my career. Thanks also to Tristan Williams for permission to include his poem.

My sincere thanks to the professionals and the admin staff of the Adult Department at the Tavistock Centre who kindly accommodated my various requests during my teaching and research.

A special thank you to Dr Mark Ardern who as consultant of an 'Old Age Psychiatric Unit' in the NHS made it possible for me to attend his team meetings, organise and run supervision groups for staff, as weell as talk to some of his patients. Also, much appreciated thanks to Paul Terry for including me as part of his team at Birkbeck College – University of London – on a course to teach care staff, to observer and listen to their institutionalised old patients, to gain some insight to their 'inner state' and emotional need.

Thanks to Judith Edwards and especially Edith White for her perceptive editing. Also, my thanks to Joe Shillito, Lauren Bailey and others involved with the assistance in the publication of this book.

My appreciation to Kaitlin Cunningham for help with computer skills.

Finally, my heartfelt and sincere thanks to all my patients who helped me gain insight and trusted me with some of their innermost feelings and thoughts. The trust and willingness of my older patients to share their secrets has been inspirational in the fruition of this book.

ABOUT THE AUTHOR

Cambridge-based *Savi McKenzie-Smith* was born in South Africa and left during her early twenties to come to the UK. Initially, she worked as a teacher with special needs children when she became aware of the importance of emotional well-being. This led to her training as a child, adolescent and adult psychoanalytic psychotherapist at the Tavistock Centre.

Her first research was based on a pioneering study of the application of the Infant Observation Method to observe institutionalised old people, to understand their emotional need – currently a part of some training courses. A further research as a PhD thesis was based on working analytically with depressed older adults, to encourage them to enhance the remainder of their lifestyle. Savi has practised, tutored, lectured at the Tavistock Centre, in the NHS, Birkbeck College and abroad. She now specialises in working with depressed older adults.